World Food

INDIA

BEVERLY LEBLANC

World Food
INDIA

p

This is a Parragon Book
This edition published in 2005

Parragon
Queen Street House
4 Queen Street
Bath BA1 1HE, UK

Created and produced by The Bridgewater Book Company Ltd.
Project Editor Emily Casey Bailey
Project Designer Michael Whitehead
Photography David Jordan
Editor Kay Halsey
Home Economist Jacqui Bellefontaine
Additional photography Max Alexander (11, 15, 22, 25, 78, 80, 96,
124, 144, 151, 196, 206, 208, 228), Adrian Bailey (100, 109, 141,
156, 203, 212, 214, 232), Jonathan Bailey (48, 52, 59, 68, 103, 239,
240, 249, 250), Caroline Jones (2, 12, 17, 18, 20, 35, 36, 56, 169,
171, 172, 189, 198, 224, 231)

ISBN: 1-40545-705-8

Printed in China

NOTES FOR THE READER

- This book uses both metric and imperial measurements. Follow
  the same units of measurement throughout; do not mix metric
  and imperial.

- All spoon measurements are level: teaspoons are assumed to be
  5 ml, and tablespoons are assumed to be 15 ml.

- Unless otherwise stated, milk is assumed to be full fat, eggs and
  individual vegetables such as potatoes are medium, and pepper
  is freshly ground black pepper.

- Recipes using raw or very lightly cooked eggs should be avoided
  by infants, the elderly, pregnant women, convalescents and
  anyone suffering from an illness.

- The times given are an approximate guide only. Preparation times
  differ according to the techniques used by different people and
  the cooking times may also vary from those given.

contents

Introduction 8
In the Indian Kitchen 26

Snacks & Starters 30
Onion Bhaji *Pyaaz Pakora* 38
Vegetarian Samosas *Aloo Mattar Samosa* 40
Golden Cauliflower Pakoras *Gobhi ka Pakora* 42
Sweet and Spicy Nuts *Khatta-Meetha Mewa* 43
Bhel Poori *Bhel Puri* 44
Khandvi *Khandvi* 47
Spicy Prawns with Cucumber *Masala Jhinga aur Kakdi* 48
Prawn and Pineapple Tikka *Jhinga aur Annanas Tikka* 51
Raita Potatoes *Aloo ka Raita* 52
Chicken Tikka *Murgh Tikka* 55
Plantain Chips *Kele ke Chips* 59
Paneer Tikka *Paneer Tikka* 60
Cocktail Crab Cakes *Kekda Tikki* 62
Onion and Tomato Salad *Cachumber* 64
Gujarat Carrot Salad *Gajar nu Salat* 65
Malabar Hill Crab Salad *Eguru Kosumalli* 66
Chilli Chickpea Salad *Chatpate Channe* 67
Memsahib's Mulligatawny Soup *Mullagatanni* 68
Rasam *Rasam* 71
Turmeric Yogurt Soup *Haldi Dahi ka Shorba* 72

Vegetable Dishes 74
Sambhar *Sambhar* 82
Dosa Masala *Masala Dosa* 84
Hot Tomato Raita *Tamattar ka Raita* 86
Spiced Balti Cabbage *Bhuni Pattagobhi* 87
Spiced Pumpkin and Coconut *Kaddu aur Nariyal ki Sabzi* 88
Parsi Scrambled Eggs *Akoori* 89
Cauliflower, Aubergine and Green Bean Korma *Sabzi ka Korma* 90
Chickpeas with Spiced Tomatoes *Chhole Tamattar* 93
Tomato-stuffed Aubergines *Bharwan Baingan Tamattari* 94
Spinach and Paneer *Saag Paneer* 99
Matar Paneer *Mattar Paneer* 100
Aloo Gobi *Aloo Gobi* 103

Vegetable Dishes (continued)

Madras Potatoes *Madrasi Aloo* 104

Okra Bhaji *Bhindi ki Sabzi* 106

Chilli-yogurt Mushrooms *Mushroom Dahiwale* 107

Green Beans with Mustard Seeds and Coconut *Frans Bean Raiwali* 109

Spinach and Lentils *Palak Daal* 110

Black Dal *Maah ki Daal* 113

Sweet-and-sour Lentils *Khatti Meethi Daal* 114

Kitchri *Khichdee* 117

Meat & Poultry Dishes 118

Lamb Biryani *Gosht Biryani* 126

Rogan Josh *Rogan Josh* 129

Lamb Pasanda *Gosht Pasanda* 130

Coriander Lamb Kebabs *Gosht Hara Kabab* 133

Sesame Lamb Chops *Champ Tilwale* 134

Lamb Dopiaza *Gosht Dopiaza* 137

Lamb Dhansak *Gosht Dhansak* 138

Lamb with Cauliflower *Gobhi Gosht* 141

Lamb Shanks Marathani *Ghati Gosht* 142

Railroad Pork and Vegetables *Sabzi Gosht* 147

Pork Vindaloo *Gosht Vindaloo* 148

Kheema Matar *Kheema Mattar* 151

Beef Madras *Madrasi Gosht* 152

Balti Beef *Bhuna Gosht* 155

Tandoori Chicken *Tandoori Murgh* 156

Butter Chicken *Murgh Makhani* 158

Quick Chicken Curry with Mushrooms and Beans *Murgh Mushroom Rasedaar* 160

Chicken Tikka Masala *Murgh Tikka Makhani* 161

Kashmiri Chicken *Murgh Kashmiri* 162

Chicken Jalfrezi *Murgh Jalfrezi* 164

Seafood Dishes 166

Tandoori Prawns *Tandoori Jhinga* 174

Mussels with Mustard Seeds and Shallots *Tissario Kadugu* 177

Steamed Fish with Coriander Chutney *Paatrani Machchi* 178

Balti Fish Curry *Machchli Masala* 181

Goan-style Seafood Curry *Goa che Nalla chi Kadi* 182

Prawn Pooris *Jhinga Puri* 185

Pickled Mackerel *Bhangde Lonchen* 186

Pomfret in Chilli Yogurt *Dahi Pamplet* 189

Fish Pakoras *Machchli Pakora* 190

Desserts & Drinks — 192

Kheer *Kheer* — 200
Payasam *Payasam* — 201
Carrot Halva *Gajar ka Halwa* — 203
Saffron and Almond Kulfi *Kesar Badaam Kulfi* — 204
Indian Bread Pudding *Shahi Tukda* — 206
Shrikhand with Pomegranate *Shrikhand Anaari* — 207
Spiced Fruit Salad *Phal ki Chaat* — 210
Salt Lassi *Namkeen Lassi* — 212
Mango Lassi *Aam ki Lassi* — 213
Masala Tea *Masalewali Chai* — 214
Pistachio and Almond Shake *Pista-Badaam Doodh* — 216
Ginger Cordial *Adrak ka Sherbet* — 217

Accompaniments — 218

Fruit and Nut Pilaf *Shahi Mewa Pullao* — 227
Lemon Rice *Nimbu Bhaat* — 228
Coconut Rice *Thengai Sadaam* — 231
Spiced Basmati Rice *Chunke hue Chawal* — 232
Naans *Naans* — 235
Chapatis *Chapatis* — 236
Parathas *Parathas* — 239
Pooris *Puris* — 240
Dosas *Dosas* — 243
Raita *Raita* — 244
Coriander Chutney *Hare Dhaniye ki Chutney* — 245
Chilli and Onion Chutney *Mirch aur Pyaaz ki Chutney* — 246
Coconut Sambal *Nariyal Sambal* — 247
Mango Chutney *Aam ki Chutney* — 248
Tamarind Chutney *Imli ki Chutney* — 249
Chilli Bon-bon *Badi Mirchi ka Meetha Achaa* — 250
Garam Masala *Garam Masala* — 251
Paneer *Paneer* — 252
Ghee *Ghee* — 253

Index — 254

INTRODUCTION

10 Indian food is as vibrant, colourful and intriguing as the country itself. The numerous and diverse regional cuisines reflect the sheer massive size of India, its huge population, its history as a trading and occupied nation and, of course, the mix of ancient religions that are practised. India's culinary traditions have been born out of great wealth and great poverty, and offer exciting flavours unlike anywhere else on earth.

The Indian subcontinent covers about 3.3 million square kilometres, stretching over 3000 kilometres from the snow-capped, towering peaks of the Himalayas southwards to the tropical plains of Tamil Nadu, bordered by the Malabar and Coromandel coasts with their elegant coconut palms. Wheat and other grains thrive in the fertile northern lands irrigated by the Ganges and Indus rivers, while rice also grows in the southern coastal regions, providing the two staple ingredients for the more than one billion Indians.

Indian cooks also utilize fish and shellfish from more than 6000 kilometres of coastline along the Arabian Sea and the Bay of Bengal, as well as numerous inland lakes, rivers and waterways. Fruit and vegetables are grown throughout the country, as well as the numerous pulses that help sustain millions of vegetarians. Sprawling spice plantations in southern India provide the flavours that make the food unique.

It's impossible to appreciate the complexity of Indian food without considering the influence of the established religions, each of which has different dietary laws. Although Westerners can read about how the cow is sacred in India, it only becomes apparent what this means in practice after observing traffic in cosmopolitan Delhi grind to a halt as a cow strolls across the street. Religion touches all aspects of secular life in India, which naturally includes food and eating customs.

Although the overwhelming majority of India's population is Hindu, the other established religions include Islam, Buddhism, Judaism, Christianity and Zoroastrianism, the Parsis' religion. This mix throws up numerous considerations for Indian cooks, or anyone cooking for Indians. Some Hindus and Sikhs are vegetarians, yet others eat all meats, except beef, and there aren't any restrictions on consuming dairy products made from cows' and water buffaloes' milk. Muslims don't eat pork. Kosher Jews don't touch pork or shellfish. Christians and Parsis eat meat, poultry, seafood and vegetables. Buddhists and Jains are strict vegetarians, with Jains even excluding all root vegetables, garlic and onion from their diets. Add to these religious taboos the fact that meat is too expensive for millions upon millions of Indians, and the result is the exciting cuisine of India, which includes an unrivalled range of vegetarian dishes.

Religion and food are also intertwined in the numerous religious festivals that dot the calendar year. The Hindu festival of lights, Divali, when Laxmi, the goddess of wealth, is prayed to, includes eating many sweetmeats while visiting families and friends. Ramadan is the Muslim month of sunrise-to-sunset fasting, and each night the fast is broken with a large

Boats drift lazily along the palm-fringed backwaters of Kerala in India's southernmost state

feast. Christians feast at Christmas on roast suckling pig and distribute marzipan sweets, while dishes such as fish fillets in a cherry tomato sauce are served at most Parsi religious festivals and weddings.

Small portions of food, such as rice or coconut in the south and small sweet milk cakes in the north, are offered with prayers to images of specific gods in Hindu homes. After the food has been blessed, a small amount of the offering is eaten in the belief that the prayers will be granted.

Indian culinary history has also been shaped by numerous outside influences. After several attempts, the Muslim Moghuls successfully invaded northern India from Persia in the sixteenth century, establishing a dynasty that lasted almost 200 years. As part of the Moghuls' sophisticated lifestyle – rich in music, elegant and tranquil gardens, beautiful architecture and exquisite fabrics – they introduced a highly refined style of cooking. Written accounts of the lavish feasts and banquets record generous hospitality and great extravagance. The Moghul tradition of using fresh and dried fruits, nuts, meat, exotic spices such as saffron and cardamom, and rich cream sauces continues today in the biryanis, pilafs, pasandas and kormas that are still appreciated around the world.

By the time Moghul power ended in the eighteenth century, European intervention and territory acquisition had already begun, adding another dimension to India's culinary history. The Portuguese, for example, desperate to control the lucrative Indian spice trade, had captured Goa, off the west coast. This gave Christianity a foothold on the subcontinent, but more importantly from the perspective of the kitchen, the Portuguese troops introduced the chilli pepper, perhaps the most common flavouring used today.

Wooden string puppets made by skilled craftsmen
are a traditional artform in western India

Indian food is popular around the world, but nowhere more so than in Britain

Although the Dutch and French also established trading posts, the dominating foreign force became the British East India Company, which eventually led to the establishment of the British Raj. Its lasting culinary legacy is in the Anglo-Indian kitchens, primarily around Kolkata, known as Calcutta at the time of British rule. It was also in part due to the constant travels to and from Britain that the exciting flavours of India became well known and appreciated abroad.

Indian food abroad
Indian food is popular around the world, but nowhere more so than in Britain. At the start of the twenty-first century, Chicken Tikka Masala (see page 161) continually tops all opinion polls of the most popular British dish, though its Indian heritage is somewhat suspect.

Punjabi and Bangladeshi chefs and restaurateurs are credited with spreading the enthusiasm for Indian food, especially in Britain, opening numerous neighbourhood restaurants in the years since Partition in 1947. And it was the Punjabi formula of serving tandoori-style recipes from home along with rich Moghul-inspired meat and rice dishes that was most successful, consequently influencing foreign impressions of Indian food. Yet, as delicious and satisfying as the standard Indian restaurant menu might be, authentic Indian cuisine offers much more.

Looking through any list of authentic Indian recipes, the one dish that won't be included is a 'curry'. This is because the word is simply an Anglicization of the Tamil word '*kari*', which can mean two things: the leaves of the *kari* plant or a

14

Although many cooks still grind spices daily, traditions are starting to change

southern Indian technique of frying vegetables with a masala called *kari podi*, hence the term 'curry powder'. By the end of the British Raj, however, the definition of the 'curry' had been expanded to mean any spicy stew-like dish served with rice and the flatbreads called chapatis, and it is now often used by Westerners to describe all Indian food. Quite a mistake!

Curry powder is anathema to Indian cooks. Instead, different combinations of spices are ground into a masala to flavour specific dishes. Although many cooks still grind spices daily, traditions are starting to change as Indian food shops sell packets of prepared masalas, though never a generic curry powder.

A culinary tour of India

To appreciate the variety of authentic Indian food, it would be necessary to travel the length and breadth of the country, ideally dining in private homes. Tourists can eat well in India, but the numerous hotel buffets generally prepare dishes that have been tailored to suit western tastes. Much of the food on offer is not much different from that available at any high-street restaurant back home.

Northern India

Rogan Josh (see page 129), Lamb Pasanda (see page 130), Tandoori Chicken (see page 156), Naans (see page 235) and other familiar Indian restaurant favourites come from northern India, which makes it an ideal starting point for a culinary tour. North India stretches from Rajasthan to Haryana, the Punjab, disputed Jammu and Kashmir along the Pakistan border, through Himachal and Uttar Pradesh and

Bihar eastwards to the remote state of Arunachal Pradesh, bordering China in the northeast. It encompasses rugged mountain ranges, mighty rivers and arid deserts.

The popular basmati and patna rices are harvested here, as are Assam and Darjeeling teas for export around the world. The Punjab is known as the 'bread basket' of India for the amount of wheat it grows, supplying local needs as well as the rest of the

country. Nowhere else in India is meat so popular as it is in this heterogeneous region. The Punjab is the home of Sikhism, and most Sikhs eat all meats except beef. The Rajputs of Rajasthan also avoid beef, but have a long tradition as warriors and hunters, so game as well as meat is part of their culinary history. In the grass-covered Himalayan foothills of Kashmir, excellent lamb is produced, which replaces goat in most local meals.

An elephant strides past a crowd waiting outside a Hindu temple complex

The Punjab is the home of tandoori cooking. The simple conical clay ovens, heated by glowing charcoal or wood in the bottom, are still shaped by hand and left to dry in the sun as they were 500 years ago when they were introduced by the invading Moghuls. The high temperature in the bottom heats the sides so that

Much of the distinctive flavour of northern cooking is from the judicious use of garam masala

food cooks quickly and remains tender on the inside. Open at the top and shaped like Ali Baba baskets, *tandoor* ovens range from 30 cm/12 inches tall to higher than an upright man. Tender marinated and spiced goat, lamb and chicken kebabs are cooked in *tandoor* ovens and served with one of the myriad pulse dishes, all called dals, and a bread almost everywhere in the Punjab and other parts of northern India.

Rice is an optional extra in the north of India, except for in Kashmir, where it replaces bread in most meals. For the rest of the region, bread accompanies every meal, be it the flatbreads chapatis or parathas, or leavened naans cooked on the side of a *tandoor* oven. *Roti*, the most basic flatbread, is also eaten by millions everyday and is served in the large communal dining halls run by Sikh temples.

Dairy products add richness to northern cooking. Ghee, the Indian form of clarified butter, is the favoured cooking fat, and yogurt is used for everything from cool, refreshing lassis to drink to tenderizing marinades for tandoori recipes. It is also curdled and pressed into paneer, the white cheese that is a prime source of protein for vegetarians. Butter is called *makhani*, lending its name to such dishes as *Murgh Makhani*, or Butter Chicken (see page 158), the popular restaurant and party dish.

Greens, such as spinach and mustard leaves, are slowly cooked to combine with different pulses or enriched with paneer or butter. The well-known *Saag Paneer* (see page 99) comes from this region.

Much of the distinctive flavour of northern cooking is from the judicious use of garam masala, a flavouring virtually unknown in the south. This traditional mix of spices is intended to warm the body from the inside.

Central India

Continuing southward, central India, made up of the predominantly vegetarian state of Gujarat on the west coast, Maharashtra, Orissa and Andhra Pradesh slightly to the south, and fish-loving Bengal on the east coast, offers many taste sensations for the foodie traveller. The food is varied and diverse, but fried seafood is enormously popular on both coasts and rice begins to replace wheat as the staple starch.

Gujarati cuisine is known first and foremost for its outstanding vegetarian food and the imaginative use of dals. Every type of pulse is utilized, including the black chickpea (*kala chana*), which is not widely known outside India. White chickpeas are equally popular and the dried variety is finely ground into besan, or gram, flour. This creamy coloured flour with a slightly earthy flavour is used to replace wheat flour in the batter for the popular potato pakoras. It's also used to make Khandvi (see page 47), the thinly rolled Italian gnocchi-like pastry that is finished with quickly fried spices and seeds. This snack is particularly popular with Jains because it doesn't contain any onion or garlic.

For a rich and creamy dessert from the region that graces religious and wedding celebration tables in all parts of the country, try Shrikhand on page 207, flavoured with ground cardamom and golden saffron.

Mumbai (formerly Bombay) has a long history as a trading port, so food in this capital city of Maharashtra has always absorbed outside influences,

Right *Fruit and vegetables for sale in Indian markets are always seasonal and locally grown*

Overleaf *The Gadi Sagar tank provides water for the desert city of Jaisalmer in Rajasthan*

Known as the 'darling of the waters', hilsa has a life cycle similar to that of salmon

with exciting, spicy results. The city's long maritime history and large number of hotels that accommodate a constant flow of foreigners means it is like a one-stop shop to sample cooking from all of India, as well as Chinese and European fare. Traditional dishes are available, but there are also many opportunities to sample modern cooking from young chefs who want to give Indian food a lighter touch.

Mumbai's Chowpatty Beach is the ultimate destination for anyone on a culinary tour who wants to sample a wide array of Indian snacks, or *chaat*, and other street food. Despite this, western fast-food outlets have started opening in Mumbai and all the other major cities with beef-free menus, but the endearing tradition of the daily delivery of home-cooked lunches for office workers doesn't look in danger of being replaced by mass-produced sandwiches or chicken burgers. Each working day, in suburbs and rural communities all around Mumbai, tiered containers called *dabbas* are filled with complete hot, fresh meals and dispatched on a late morning train to the city. As thousands of the identical-looking *dabbas* arrive at the main railroad terminus, teams of *dabba wallas* collect and deliver them to the correct desks in offices across the city with miraculous accuracy. It is an amazing feat of organization, then after lunch the process is repeated in reverse, with the empty *dabbas* arriving at the correct homes. Who in their right mind would want to swap a spiced dal, such as lentils with spinach, a vegetable dish, rice, a fresh chapati and a selection of flavoursome chutneys and a raita for a mass-produced chicken burger?

Agriculture is the major source of income for Maharashtrians, and for more than a century Mumbai's noisy and colourful Victorian Crawford Market, renamed Jyotiba Phule Market, was the city's largest wholesale fruit and vegetable market. Produce from all of India passed through the French Gothic-style building. However, recently the market has moved out of the centre in an attempt to relieve inner-city congestion. The deep-sea Koli fishermen, with their brightly coloured boats, provide a steady supply of fresh seafood for grilling, frying and baking, and the highly prized pomfret comes from along the Mumbai coast. Typically, Maharashtrian food, described on Indian menus as *Marathani*, includes peanuts and cashew nuts, such as in the Lamb Shanks Marathani recipe on page 142.

Mumbai, with its Towers of Silence, is also home to India's main Parsi community, known for their deliciously spiced food. Try the Lamb Dhansak recipe on page 138 for a traditional Parsi dish that is often served with glasses of ice-cold beer. Brown rice is the usual accompaniment, but plain basmati rice is also suitable. Another typically Parsi dish is scrambled eggs given a spicy edge with chopped green chillies and fresh coriander: a better wake-up call than a cup of coffee in the morning.

Travelling eastwards, fish is king in Bengal where the Ganges and the rivers flowing down from the Himalayas reach the Bay of Bengal. Many Bengalis consider a meal incomplete if it doesn't include fish. Hilsa, or *elish*, a member of the shad family, is the most popular species. Known as the 'darling of the waters', hilsa has a life cycle similar to that of salmon: the shimmering silver-grey fish begins life in the sea, spawns in the estuary where the rivers meet the Bay of Bengal, then begins a slow journey up the

There are as many as 5 million holy men in India, many of whom grow their hair long to emulate Lord Shiva

A working camel marches through a busy street scene in Jaipur in Rajasthan

rivers to the north of the country. It is on this northward journey, after monsoon season, that Bengali fishermen set out at night to make their catch. The only problem with this delicacy, which can be cooked like herring, shad or salmon, is the tremendous number of bones. Foreigners as well as Indians have to use their fingers to eat hilsa.

The annual monsoon rains, when they come, are strongest in Bengal, producing ideal conditions for farmers. In a good year, tropical fruits thrive and bananas, coconut, pineapples and pomelos are plentiful here. The fertile soil also yields tea, coffee,

corn, tapioca, cocoa and a host of spices. The British introduced the potato, from which Anglo-Indians have created numerous recipes, and pumpkin is another favourite vegetable. Of course, coconut is abundant along the coast and finds its way into all sorts of foods from snacks to the sweetmeats Kolkata is famed for.

Sugar cane also thrives in the Bengali climate, so sweetness works its way into savoury dishes as well as sweetmeats. Try the Sweet-and-sour Lentils recipe on page 114 to sample this intriguing mix of sweet and savoury.

Like Mumbai, Kolkata offers an amazing range of *chaat* and street foods, with hawkers pushing carts along the crowded thoroughfares. The city also has a tradition of café society, where intellectuals and academics meet to talk over cups of Masala Tea (see page 214) and a steady stream of sweetmeats.

Bengali seafood, dal and vegetable dishes are given their regional character by being cooked with mustard oil and flavoured with *panch phoron*, the masala of the region. It is made by toasting equal quantities of mustard, cumin, fennel, fenugreek and nigella seeds, then used whole or ground into powder.

Hyderabad, in the centre of Andhra Pradesh, has a long history of scholarship and is also known for its extravagant saffron-infused meat and rice biryanis, which once graced the ruling Nizams' tables. Like the Moghul rulers before them, the extraordinarily wealthy Muslim Nizams presided over lavish feasts and banquets. The city is a must-stop for anyone on a culinary tour of India. The slightly streamlined Lamb Biryani on page 126 has been adapted for modern tastes, but it is still a fragrant and flavoursome mix of basmati rice, spices – garam masala, cinnamon, cumin, chilli and turmeric – and meltingly tender lamb. Coastal food in Andhra Pradesh includes spiced fish and prawns cooked in sesame and coconut oils and vegetables, such as okra, flavoured with fresh herbs and spices.

Southern India
Spices and seafood are two of the culinary joys of any visit to southern India and both are abundant. Sunny, palm-fringed Kerala, Karnataka and Tamil Nadu offer the lightest food in India with spicy flavours.

Spices are not only a flavouring in south India. Spice growing is big business and peppercorns were once known as 'black gold'. Kochi (formerly Cochin) is the centre of India's spice trade, and the aromas of cardamom, coriander, cumin, cinnamon and vanilla wafting out of warehouses scent the air in the old town with its winding narrow streets and antique shops. Any visit to southern India should include

Spices and seafood are two of the culinary joys of any visit to southern India and both are abundant

a stop at a spice plantation to view favourite flavourings growing in their natural habitat and taste them at their freshest.

The pale green cardamoms, red and green chillies, curry leaves, mustard seeds and golden turmeric used in southern Indian cooking give the food a vibrant appearance as well as flavour. Many traditional dishes also have a distinctive sharp, sour taste derived from tamarind pulp.

Fresh coconut plantations stretch as far as the eyes can see in this part of India, and coconut trees also grow easily in domestic gardens in this tropical climate, so coconut is also a popular, everyday flavouring that finds its way into dishes from snacks through to desserts. Boat tours along Kerala's waterways can also include a stop at a coconut plantation to sample just-off-the-tree coconut flesh and milk: much milder than when coconuts have aged during travel to western supermarkets.

Rice is the predominant starch in the south and the natural partner to serve with the soup-like dals, such as Sambhar (see page 82), which is eaten by millions every day. Rice is also used to make the pancakes and steamed rice cakes that are unique to the region: fermented rice and black lentils are ground into a batter for thin, crisp Dosas (see page 243), and steamed flying-saucer-looking *idlis* are served for breakfasts, often with a highly spiced dal that starts the day with a kick. *Upama*, a steamed semolina cake flavoured with curry leaves, mustard leaves and chilli, is another rice cake eaten at breakfast or as a snack.

Kerala, with its harmonious mix of Hindus, Muslims, Christians and a Jewish community in Kochi, has an

Enjoying an Indian meal in India is very different from dining in western Indian restaurants

interesting cuisine. An impressive variety of fish and shellfish, from the Arabian Sea as well as the intercoastal network of waterways, is always available, but dals and even beef are served here. For seafood with a just-caught flavour, try one of the ramshackle eating huts across from the Chinese fishing nets along the harbour at Fort Kochi.

The hot, chilli-spiced food characteristically prepared around Chennai (formerly Madras) is now mistakenly taken to represent all Indian cooking to people who prefer milder food. The liberal use of chillies, however, is designed to counter the tropical heat. As the chillies warm the body from the inside, perspiration cools the body on the outside. The Beef Madras recipe on page 152 showcases the popular flavour combination of chillies and coconut.

Cashew nuts flourish in the long, dry growing season in Karnataka, as well as in Goa and Kerala, so anyone who enjoys them in small amounts elsewhere because of the cost, can really indulge here. Bowls are constantly refilled in hotel bars. In March, visit the markets to see the freshly harvested nuts still attached to the green fruit.

At the southern tip of Tamil Nadu the numerous temple cities offer some of India's most fascinating architecture and outstanding vegetarian food, based on spicy dal stews, rice and fresh-tasting chutneys. Coffee, a cash crop, is also drunk throughout the day here, much like spiced tea in other parts of India.

Eating the Indian way

Enjoying an Indian meal in India is very different from dining in western Indian restaurants, even if the dishes are identical. The concept of serving a series of courses is alien to most Indians. Instead the entire meal, including dessert, is presented at once. The traditional method for this is to serve the different dishes in small bowls called *katoris* on a round metal plate called a *thali,* which can be as utilitarian as stainless steel, as elaborate as decorated gold or silver, or as charming as a large banana leaf in the south. As styles change, however, this is becoming more a method of restaurant presentation than one used for family meals. Today home meals are just as likely to be served western 'family style', with all the dishes in the centre of the table for everyone to help themselves.

When an Indian cook plans a *thali* meal, he or she first decides the main dish, be it chicken, meat or a dal. Next, a vegetable dish with complementary flavours and a raita will be decided on, then the type of rice and/or bread and chutneys will be selected. As with a western meal, the cook strives for a combination of textures and flavours as well as colours. A 'veg' *thali*, for example, might consist of a dal, with two or three vegetable dishes, such as Okra Bhaji (see page 106), Matar Paneer (see page 100) and Raita Potatoes (see page 52), along with one or two chutneys, arranged around a mound of rice in the centre. A chapati might be added as well.

The Indian skill of eating with their fingers takes great practice. All Indians agree that only the right hand is used, but that is where the consensus ends. Northerners use only the very tips of their fingers to tear a piece of bread to scoop up bite-size portions of food, then watch in horror as southerners use their fingers to scoop up their food.

A woman sells fresh fruit on Goa's popular Benaulim Beach

In the Indian kitchen

It has never been easier for non-Indian cooks to capture the diverse and fragrant flavours of Indian food. Once exotic and difficult-to-source ingredients are now commonplace in supermarkets.

Banana leaves Southern Indian food served on these large, glossy, dark green leaves looks as stunning as it tastes. The leaves can also be wrapped around food before cooking. The leaves are sold fresh in Indian and other Asian food shops.

Basmati rice (basmati chaaval) Grown in the foothills of the Himalayas, this is the long-grain rice used in recipes in this book. It is valued around the world for its delicate fragrance and silky grains that remain separate during cooking. Outside of India, basmati rice is synonymous with Indian food, but more than 20 varieties of rice are grown and used within the country. Consequently, basmati is often saved for special occasions and celebrations. This is the rice to use for lavish biryanis and pilafs.

Basmati rice traditionally requires extensive rinsing and soaking before cooking, but some supermarket brands recommend skipping this step. Always read the packet before cooking.

To prepare perfect basmati rice, rinse 55 g/2 oz per person under cold water until the water runs clear. Put the rice in a bowl with water to cover and leave to soak for 30 minutes. Drain the rice and put in a heavy-based saucepan with a tight-fitting lid. Add enough water to cover (the exact amount does not matter) and a large pinch of salt and bring to the boil, then boil, uncovered, for 6 minutes. Drain in a sieve or colander that will fit in the pan, but do not rinse. Put a shallow layer of water in the bottom of the pan and put the sieve or colander on top, without letting the rice touch the water. Cover with the lid and steam over a medium heat for about 4 minutes. Fluff with a fork and serve, stirring in extra salt if necessary.

Coconut (nariyal) Considered the 'fruit of the gods', coconuts are important in Hindu religious ceremonies, as well as to the kitchens of southern India and Goa. The creamy white flesh and thin, cloudy coconut water are used in cooking and as snacks. Coconut cream and the thinner coconut milk are available in cans or can be made by soaking freshly grated coconut flesh in boiling water. If using canned coconut cream, be sure to buy the unsweetened variety.

The quickest way to add a rich coconut flavour to curries without the fuss of opening a fresh coconut is to dissolve a specified amount of creamed coconut in boiling water. Pressed bars of white creamed coconut are sold in supermarkets.

Coriander (hara dhaniya) Coriander leaves are to Indian cooks what parsley is to western cooks. They add a bright green colourful garnish to many dishes and a sharp flavour to breads, rice, chutneys, salads and many drinks. The roots can also be finely chopped and added to other ingredients.

Curry leaves (kadhi patta) These thin, pointed green leaves, which look like miniature bay leaves, grow on trees native to India and Sri Lanka. They are so called because the whole tree gives off a 'curry' aroma. The leaves are often fried and added at the end of cooking for a garnish, giving an aromatic, slightly bitter flavour to primarily southern Indian dishes. Buy fresh in Indian food shops or dried at supermarkets.

Fenugreek (methi) Small, irregular-shaped fenugreek seeds are one of the flavourings included in commercial curry powders, but they are less used in Indian masalas. Fenugreek seeds are added to dals to help counter flatulence. The seeds are often fried at the beginning of a recipe, but take care because they taste bitter if overcooked. Fresh fenugreek leaves can be cooked like spinach. Ground fenugreek and fenugreek seeds are sold at supermarkets. Fresh and dried leaves are available from Indian food shops.

Ginger (adrak) Anyone who wants to add an authentic flavour to their Indian cooking should stock up on this knobbly rhizome. The warm, spicy taste is essential to so many meat, poultry and fish dishes, as well as numerous vegetarian favourites. For the best flavour, buy fresh ginger with a tight, smooth skin. A wrinkled skin is an indication that the flesh is drying out. Store in a covered container in the refrigerator. Ginger is often ground into a paste before cooking, and many of the recipes in this book start with frying a paste made from ginger and garlic.

To make the **Garlic and Ginger Paste**, blend together equal quantities of garlic and ginger. Because the quantities required are often too small to process in a blender or food processor, it makes sense to make a larger quantity and store it in a sealed jar in the refrigerator for up to 3 weeks, or in the freezer for up to 1 month. Alternatively, you can grind the required amount for a specific recipe using a spice grinder or pestle and mortar.

Jaggery (gur) A by-product in the production of sugar from sugar cane, this sweetener is used in place of sugar in many Indian recipes, especially sweets. It is sold in a cone or barrel shape in Indian food shops. Soft light brown or demerara sugar can be used instead.

Mint (pudina) Introduced to India by the Persians, this fresh-tasting herb is particularly popular in northern India, where it garnishes rich meat and poultry dishes. Fresh mint also flavours many chutneys, raitas and drinks.

Mustard oil (sarson ka tel) A popular cooking oil with a strong, pungent flavour. To counter the pronounced flavour, many recipes begin by heating the oil until it is very hot and then leaving it to cool before reheating and adding other ingredients. Look for this in Indian food shops and some supermarkets.

Silver foil (varak) Indian desserts and sweets are elevated to special status with a decoration of edible silver dust pressed into ultra-thin sheets more delicate than kitchen foil. Easy to use, this shimmering decoration is sold in Indian food shops.

Tamarind (imli) When an Indian dish has a distinctive and pronounced sour flavour, such as Sweet-and-sour Lentils (see page 114), there is a good chance it includes one form or another of this pulp taken from tamarind pods. Supermarkets sell pots of ready-to-use tamarind paste or you can buy tamarind as a compressed slab that needs to be reconstituted with boiling water, then strained.

Yogurt (dahi) There are countless uses for natural yogurt in the Indian kitchen. It is used as a tenderizer and a souring agent, as well as the main ingredient in numerous raitas and some chutneys. Yogurt, referred to as 'curd' in Indian recipes, is made from buffalo milk and served in one form or another at most Indian meals. The cool and refreshing Salt Lassi (see page 212) is made with yogurt, and in some regions every meal is ended with a bowl of yogurt. For a special indulgent dessert, try Shrikhand (see page 207), strained yogurt delicately flavoured with cardamom and saffron.

In the Indian spice box

Indian food without spices is like a garden without flowers. Spices are the essence of Indian cooking. A walk through any Indian spice market assaults the senses on two fronts: the heady aroma is exotic and tantalizing, and the kaleidoscope of colours is dazzling. Mounds of vibrant red ground chillies, golden tamarind, pale green cardamom pods, jet-black nigella seeds, grey poppy seeds and creamy sesame spilling out of burlap sacks can give the visit an almost magical feel.

Curry powder as such is not used in India. Instead, Indian cooks skilfully combine spices to give each dish its own character with a distinctive flavour and colour. Prepared spice mixtures called masalas are sold in India just as they are in the West, but the tradition of combining and grinding spices for each meal is still widely practised.

Below are the spices that contribute an authentic flavour to the recipes in this book. Ready-ground spices are convenient, but they lose their flavour more quickly than whole spices that are ground as they are required.

Asafoetida (hing) It's not for nothing that this finely ground resin is known as 'the devil's dung', because the pungent sulphurous aroma is very off-putting until it is cooked. Indian cooks include asafoetida in vegetables, pulses, pickles and other dishes for its digestive qualities, and Hindu Brahmins and Jains use it to replace the flavour of forbidden garlic and onion. Asafoetida is used only in small amounts and it is sold in small, airtight containers in supermarkets or Indian food shops.

Cardamom (elaichi) Known as the 'queen of spices' (black pepper is the 'king'), green cardamom is one of the most popular flavourings in Indian cooking, used in both savoury and sweet dishes as well as drinks. The delicate, sweet aroma comes from the tiny seeds contained in the small, smooth pods. Even though the whole pods are often included in dishes they are not meant to be eaten, although chewing cardamom pods as a breath freshener dates from Moghul times. Black cardamom has a much heavier, pronounced flavour and is only used in savoury recipes. Cardamom is widely available in supermarkets, ground or in pods, which retain their freshness for longer.

Chillies, green and red (hari mirch and lal mirch) Synonymous as chillies are with Indian food, they are relative newcomers to the Indian spice box, having been introduced by the Portuguese. More than 20 varieties of chillies grow in India now, with colours ranging from white and saffron yellow to the more familiar red and green ones. Green chillies are unripe red chillies.

Unfortunately, it is difficult to tell how hot a chilli is by appearance only. As a general rule, the smaller and redder a chilli, the hotter it will be, although experience is a better guide. The amount of heat any particular chilli adds to a dish depends on whether or not it is deseeded. The more seeds left in, the hotter the dish will be. Dried red chillies have a very concentrated flavour and should only be used in small amounts.

Chilli powder Kashmiri chillies are the dark red chillies that grow in the northern region of Kashmir. They are mild tasting and are valued for the vibrant red colour they add to dishes such as Rogan Josh (see page 129) and Tandoori Chicken (see page 156), rather than for their flavour. Look for this chilli powder in Indian food shops. Cayenne chilli powder, available in all supermarkets, is the variety to use for heat rather than colour.

Cinnamon (dalchini) As in other countries, Indian cooks use this ground spice or the rolled, thin quills of the cinnamon tree bark to flavour sweet and savoury dishes and drinks. Cinnamon is one of the essential spices in Garam Masala (see page 251), used to flavour so many northern curries and rice dishes. Toasting cinnamon in a dry pan before adding it to other ingredients helps to intensify its flavour.

Cloves (laung) More frequently used whole than ground in Indian cooking, these dried flowerbuds have a strong aromatic flavour that can be overpowering if used in abundance or chewed. Cloves feature in northern Indian savoury and sweet recipes, and are used in *paan*, the mix of spices and leaves that is sold on many street corners as a mouth freshener.

Coriander (dhaniya) One of the unmistakable savoury flavours of Indian food is ground roasted coriander seeds. The seeds, which taste very different from the vibrant green leaves of the fresh herb, are round with very thin ridges and easily ground in a spice blender or using a pestle and mortar. They are sold as seeds or a ground powder.

Cumin (jeera) Popular with cooks in all regions of India, cumin is prized for its distinctive, strong flavour and digestive qualities. Many recipes start with frying the thin, slightly elongated seeds in hot oil to intensify the flavour and help spread it throughout the dish, but watch closely as they can burn and become bitter tasting in a matter of seconds. Brown cumin seeds, familiar to cooks throughout the West, are readily available, but black cumin seeds (*kala jeera*) are found in Indian food shops.

Ground mango (amchoor powder) A powder made from green mangoes and used as a meat tenderizer, to sour dishes or in chaat masala. It is available in Indian food shops.

Mustard seeds (rai) Tiny round black, brown and yellow mustard seeds are used throughout India. They are hot and spicy when raw, but are often fried in hot oil until they jump to temper their flavour. Black and brown mustard seeds can be used interchangeably. They are sold in supermarkets.

Nigella seeds (kalonji) Also known as black onion seeds (although they have nothing to do with onions), these small dark-black seeds look like tiny chips of coal and are added to fish, pickles, naans, rice and pulse dishes. Their flavour is nutty and peppery.

Saffron (kesar) The most expensive spice in the world, these thin threads come from the dried stamens of the crocus flower and are so costly because the stamens are hand-picked. Indian saffron is grown in Kashmir and used to add a brilliant golden colour and a distinctive, slightly musky taste to many Indian dishes, mostly those from the north. Used since Moghul times, saffron is rarely missing from such classic dishes as Lamb Biryani (see page 126) and special desserts. Indian 'saffron' that seems reasonably priced is more likely to actually be safflower, which, although it adds an orange-yellow tint to other ingredients, doesn't have any flavour.

Turmeric (haldi) The instant sunshine of many Indian dishes. Turmeric, a member of the ginger family, adds a golden yellow colour and a pungent flavour to meat, seafood, pulses and vegetable dishes. The ground version is sold in all supermarkets, but for the fresh or dry rhizomes go to a large Indian food shop.

SNACKS &
STARTERS

32 Street food is popular throughout Asia, but nowhere more so than in India. Eating on the go from dawn to dusk is part of daily life for many Indians. Wherever people congregate, especially in the overcrowded cities and in markets or bazaars, at busy intersections, outside shops, at train and bus stations and taxi ranks, there will be at least one person selling bags of snack mixes called *bhujiyas* (known outside India generically as Bombay mix) or squatting over makeshift heat sources cooking kebabs, frying pakoras or samosas, or pushing fruit through a juicer for fresh drinks.

The snack sellers' cries, the sizzling hot oil and the mixed scents of spices and dust are all part of the backdrop to so many Indian experiences.

Small, savoury Indian snacks are called *chaat*, which comes from the Hindi word meaning 'to lick'. This is because *chaat* are considered 'finger-licking good'. They can be enjoyed hot or cold, and are chilli hot and spicy to taste. *Chaat* are inexpensive, varied and usually a mix of tantalizing flavours. In other words, they are perfect for munching while walking along and chatting with friends.

Of course, it is easy to over-romanticize Indian street food, but much of it is good and satisfying, and the choices are endless. The ingenious, resourceful army of India's street cooks take the place of western fast-food outlets, which are still few and far between in Indian cities and nonexistent in rural areas. The exciting, varied tradition of Indian street food also survives because in many overcrowded city dwellings kitchen space is limited, if it exists at all.

For many, Indian snack and street-food culture reaches its height at Mumbai's Chowpatty Beach. In a city as densely populated as Mumbai, the beach's open space and amusement rides with their bright garish lights serve as a magnet for fast-food cooks and hungry patrons alike as the sun begins to set. Bhel Poori (see page 44), a jumbled mix of spiced diced potatoes, puffed rice and ultra-thin sev noodles, tempered with a mixture of sour tamarind chutney, spicy and refreshing coriander chutney and a dollop of yogurt, is often cited as the best example of a uniquely Indian *chaat*. Each of the open-air vendors offers a unique recipe, but whichever one is sampled it will be an unmistakable taste of Mumbai. On hot, steamy nights, courting couples and families with young children relax and cool off with a creamy Indian ice cream called Kulfi, such as the version flavoured with saffron and almonds on page 204.

And to drink with *chaat*? Masala Tea (see page 214) is a natural choice as Indians seem to drink it all day long, but a Salt Lassi (see page 212) and Mango Lassi (see page 213) are also popular. Or open an ice-cold

Small, savoury Indian snacks are called chaat, *which comes from the Hindi word meaning 'to lick'*

34

Soups are also not a traditional part of Indian meals, but were introduced by the British during the Raj

bottle of one of the Indian beers that are now available around the world.

Serving a separate first course is not a traditional part of Indian family meals, so it is with a certain amount of latitude that Indian restaurant menus outside the country feature the most popular Indian *chaat* and other street food as 'starters'. Onion Bhaji (see page 38), Golden Cauliflower Pakoras (see page 42), Vegetarian Samosas (see page 40) and Chicken Tikka (see page 55) are all examples of popular Indian street food.

Soups are also not a traditional part of Indian meals, but were introduced by the British during the Raj. Memsahib's Mulligatawny Soup (see page 68), for example, is a legacy of British rule. Missing the soups from home, British cooks took Rasam (see page 71), a spicy Tamil broth, added mutton to make it more substantial and called the result 'Mulligatawny', which loosely translates as 'pepper water'. Try both recipes to appreciate the similarities and differences.

Most of the recipes in this chapter illustrate the versatility of Indian snacks. Munch these dishes as snacks throughout the day, serve them before a more substantial main course or with chilled cocktails before dinner. For snack ideas from other chapters, try Dosa Masala (see page 84), Parsi Scrambled Eggs (see page 89) and Fish Pakoras (see page 190).

Detail of a door arch in Jaipur's City Palace, which is famous for its elaborate art and architecture

Overleaf *The beautiful Pushkar Lake in Rajasthan is overlooked by grand buildings*

onion bhaji
pyaaz pakora

There can't be many Indian restaurants, in India or elsewhere, that don't feature this popular snack, or chaat, *on the menu. Wherever you are in India, you'll find street vendors frying bhajis and other snacks in large, black wok-like vessels called kadhais. In your kitchen, however, a large, heavy-based saucepan, wok or deep-fat fryer will do the job just as efficiently.*

MAKES 12

140 g/5 oz besan or gram flour

1 tsp salt

1 tsp ground cumin

1 tsp ground turmeric

1 tsp bicarbonate of soda

$1/2$ tsp chilli powder

2 tsp lemon juice

2 tbsp vegetable or groundnut oil, plus
   extra for deep-frying

2–8 tbsp water

2 onions, thinly sliced

2 tsp coriander seeds, lightly crushed

lemon wedges, to serve

1 Sift the besan flour, salt, cumin, turmeric, bicarbonate of soda and chilli powder into a large bowl. Add the lemon juice and the oil, then very gradually stir in just enough water until a batter similar to single cream forms. Mix in the onions and coriander seeds.

2 Heat enough oil for deep-frying* in a kadhai, wok, deep-fat fryer or large, heavy-based saucepan until it reaches 180°C/350°F, or until a cube of bread browns in 30 seconds. Without overcrowding the pan, drop in spoonfuls of the onion mixture and fry for 2 minutes, then use tongs to flip the bhajis over and continue frying for a further 2 minutes, or until golden brown.

3 Immediately remove the bhajis from the oil and drain well on crumpled kitchen paper. Keep the bhajis warm while you continue frying the remaining batter. Serve hot with lemon wedges.

*cook's tip

As with all deep-fried food, the fine line between light crispiness and greasiness depends on keeping the oil at the correct temperature while the bhajis are frying. If it is too low, the bhajis will be greasy; too hot, and the coating will burn while the onions remain raw. This is why you should cook the bhajis in batches and let the oil return to the correct temperature between batches. If you do lots of deep-fat frying, it is worth investing in a thermometer.

40 vegetarian samosas
aloo mattar samosa

It takes a little practice and patience to get the hang of shaping these triangular-shaped pastries, but after you've rolled out and filled a couple you will become as proficient as India's seemingly endless army of street cooks. 'Veg' or 'non-veg' samosas are fried and sold at every street market and busy intersection.

MAKES 14

250 g/9 oz plain flour

1/2 tsp salt

40 g/1 1/2 oz Ghee (see page 253) or butter, melted

1/2 tbsp lemon juice

100–125 ml/3 1/2–4 fl oz cold water

for the filling*

55 g/2 oz Ghee (see page 253) or 4 tbsp vegetable
  or groundnut oil

1 onion, very finely chopped

2 garlic cloves, crushed

1 potato, very finely diced

2 carrots, very finely chopped

2 tsp mild, medium or hot curry powder, to taste

1 1/2 tsp ground coriander

1 tsp ground turmeric

1 fresh green chilli, deseeded and finely chopped

1 tsp salt

1/2 tsp black mustard seeds

300 ml/10 fl oz water

100 g/3 1/2 oz frozen peas

55 g/2 oz cauliflower florets, broken into the
  smallest florets possible

vegetable or groundnut oil, for frying

fresh coriander leaves, to garnish

1 To make the filling, melt the ghee in a kadhai, wok or large frying pan over a medium-high heat. Add the onion and garlic and fry for 5-8 minutes until soft but not brown.

2 Stir in the potato and carrot and continue frying, stirring occasionally, for 5 minutes. Stir in the curry powder, coriander, turmeric, chilli, salt and mustard seeds. Pour in the water and bring to the boil. Reduce the heat to very low and simmer, uncovered, for about 15 minutes, stirring occasionally. Add the peas and cauliflower florets and continue simmering until all the vegetables are tender and the liquid evaporates. Remove from the heat and set aside.

3 Meanwhile, to make the pastry, sift the flour and salt into a bowl. Make a well in the centre, add the ghee and lemon juice and work them into the flour with your fingertips. Gradually add the water until the mixture comes together to form a soft dough.

4 Tip the dough on to the work surface and knead for about 10 minutes until smooth. Shape into a ball, cover with a damp tea towel and leave to rest for about 15 minutes.

5 To shape the dough, divide into 7 equal pieces. Work with 1 piece at a time and keep the pieces you aren't working with covered with a tea towel. Roll the piece you are working with into a 20-cm/8-inch round on a lightly greased work surface, then cut in half to make 2 equal semicircles. Continue to cut out 12 more semicircles.

6 Working with one semicircle at a time, wet the edges with water. Place about 2 teaspoons of the filling on the dough, just off centre. Fold one side into

the centre, covering the filling. Fold the other side in the opposite direction, overlapping the first fold to form a cone shape. Wet the open edge with more water and press down to seal. Cover with a damp tea towel while you continue to assemble the remaining samosas.

7 Heat about 2.5 cm/1 inch of oil in a kadhai, wok or large heavy-based saucepan until it reaches 180°C/350°F, or until a cube of bread browns in 30 seconds. Fry the samosas in batches for 2–3 minutes,

flipping them over once, until golden brown, then drain well on crumpled kitchen paper. These are best served warm with coriander leaves to garnish and a chutney, but are also good eaten at room temperature.

*cook's tip

If you prefer 'non-veg' samosas, use the Kheema Matar (see page 151) recipe as a filling, simmering the mixture in an uncovered pan until it is dry.

42

golden cauliflower pakoras
gobhi ka pakora

These golden, crisp fritters appear on restaurant menus in the West, while in India they are more likely to be prepared in homes as part of a meal or as a snack, rather than being cooked on the street.

SERVES 4

vegetable or groundnut oil, for deep-frying

400 g/14 oz cauliflower florets

for the batter

140 g/5 oz besan or gram flour

2 tsp ground coriander

1 tsp Garam Masala (see page 251)

1 tsp salt

$^1/_2$ tsp ground turmeric

pinch of chilli powder

15 g/$^1/_2$ oz Ghee (see page 253), melted, or 1 tbsp
    vegetable or groundnut oil

1 tsp lemon juice

150 ml/5 fl oz cold water

2 tsp nigella seeds

1 To make the batter*, stir the besan flour, coriander, garam masala, salt, turmeric and chilli powder into a large bowl. Make a well in the centre, add the ghee and lemon juice with 2 tablespoons of the water, and stir together to make a thick batter.

2 Slowly beat in enough of the remaining water with an electric hand-held mixer or a whisk to make a smooth batter about the same thickness as double cream. Stir in the nigella seeds. Cover the bowl and set aside to stand for at least 30 minutes.

3 When you are ready to fry, heat enough oil for deep-frying in a kadhai, wok, deep-fat fryer or large heavy-based saucepan until it reaches 180°C/350°F, or until a cube of bread browns in 30 seconds. Dip one cauliflower floret at a time into the batter and let any excess batter fall back into the bowl, then drop it into the hot oil. Add a few more dipped florets, without overcrowding the pan, and fry for about 3 minutes, or until golden brown and crisp.

4 Use a slotted spoon to remove the fritters from the oil and drain well on crumpled kitchen paper. Continue frying until all the cauliflower florets and batter have been used. Serve the hot fritters with a chutney for dipping.

*cook's tip
You can make the batter a day ahead and refrigerate overnight, but let it return to room temperature and beat it well before you use it.

sweet and spicy nuts
khatta-meetha mewa

After a long day's sightseeing in the pulsating heat of Mumbai, a hotel's cocktail lounge can be a tranquil refuge and you will almost certainly be served a bowl of cashew nuts or almonds to nibble on with a cooling drink. Enjoy this spicy combination with an ice-cold beer or Salt Lassi (see page 212).

MAKES 450 G/1 LB

300 g/10¹/₂ oz caster sugar

1 tsp sea salt

2 tbsp mild, medium or hot curry powder, to taste

1 tsp ground turmeric

1 tsp ground coriander

pinch of chilli powder

450 g/1 lb mixed whole blanched almonds
  and shelled cashew nuts*

vegetable or groundnut oil, for deep-frying

1 Mix the sugar, salt, curry powder, turmeric, coriander and chilli powder together in a large bowl, then set aside.

2 Meanwhile, bring a large saucepan of water to the boil. Add the almonds and cashews and blanch for 1 minute, then tip them into a sieve to drain and shake off as much of the excess water as possible. Immediately toss the nuts with the sugar and spices.

3 Heat enough oil for deep-frying in a kadhai, wok, deep-fat fryer or large heavy-based saucepan to 180°C/350°F, or until a cube of bread browns in 30 seconds. Use a slotted spoon to remove the nuts from the spice mixture, leaving the spicy mixture behind in the bowl, then drop the nuts into the hot oil.

Fry them for 3–4 minutes, stirring occasionally and watching carefully because they can burn quickly, until they turn golden.

4 Remove the nuts from the oil with the slotted spoon and toss them in the remaining spice mixture. Tip the nuts into a sieve and shake off the excess spices, then leave to cool completely and crisp up. Store in an airtight container for up to a week.

*cook's tip
Although pecans and walnuts are not often served in India, they also taste good prepared with this spicy mixture.

44

bhel poori
bhel puri

In Mumbai, this is a popular street chaat, unbeatable for munching on hot, steamy nights walking along Chowpatty Beach. No two vendors are likely to prepare identical mixtures, but whichever one you buy it will include puffed rice and potatoes. The quantities here are a suggestion and can easily be increased or decreased to suit your personal taste.

SERVES 4–6

salt

300 g/10¹/₂ oz new potatoes

200 g/7 oz canned chickpeas, rinsed and very
 well drained

100 g/3¹/₂ oz sev noodles*

55 g/2 oz puffed rice

4 tbsp raisins

2 tbsp chopped fresh coriander

1 tbsp fennel seeds, toasted and cooled

12 mini Pooris (see page 240), crushed

4 tbsp natural yogurt

Tamarind Chutney (see page 249)

Coriander Chutney (see page 245)

for the chaat masala

1 tbsp coriander seeds

1 tbsp cumin seeds

1 tsp black peppercorns

2 dried red chillies

1 Bring a large saucepan of salted water to the boil and cook the potatoes for 12–15 minutes until tender. Drain and run under cold water to cool, then peel and cut into 5-mm/¹/₄-inch dice. Cover and chill for at least 30 minutes.

2 Meanwhile, to make the chaat masala, heat a dry frying pan over a high heat. Add the coriander and cumin seeds, peppercorns and chillies and stir around until they give off their aroma. Immediately tip them out of the pan to stop the cooking, watching closely because the cumin seeds burn quickly. Grind the toasted spice mixture in a spice grinder or pestle and mortar.

3 Use your hands to toss together the potatoes, chickpeas, sev noodles, puffed rice, raisins, coriander, fennel seeds and crushed mini pooris. Sprinkle with the chaat masala and toss again.

4 Divide the mixture among small serving bowls or place in one large bowl and drizzle with the yogurt and chutneys to taste. It is best eaten straight away so it doesn't become soggy.

*cook's tip

For an authentic taste and texture, look for bags of sev noodles in Indian food shops. They are small pieces of extra-thin noodles, often included in Bombay Mix recipes.

Served at weddings and various religious festivals, these thin, delicate besan flour rolls make an appetizing canapé with cocktails or dry white wine.

khandvi

MAKES 16 ROLLS

85 g/3 oz besan or gram flour

1 tsp ground ginger

1 tsp salt

$^1/_2$ tsp ground turmeric

$^1/_4$ tsp chilli powder, or to taste

450 ml/16 fl oz water

175 ml/6 fl oz natural yogurt

1 tbsp lemon juice

for the garnish

2 tbsp vegetable or groundnut oil

$^1/_2$ tbsp black mustard seeds

$^1/_2$ tbsp sesame seeds, toasted

1 fresh green chilli, deseeded and finely
  chopped (optional)

$^1/_2$ tbsp finely chopped fresh coriander

1 Sift the besan flour, ginger, salt, turmeric and chilli powder together into a bowl and make a well in the centre. Whisk the water, yogurt and lemon juice together, then pour into the well in the dry ingredients and whisk until a smooth batter forms.

2 Rinse the widest and deepest saucepan you have with cold water, then pour in the batter. Place over a high heat and bring to the boil, stirring constantly. Reduce the heat and continue simmering and stirring for about 30 minutes, or until the liquid evaporates and the mixture is thick.

3 Meanwhile, lightly grease a shallow, square 30-cm/12-inch baking tray*. Pour the mixture into the baking tray and use a wet spatula to spread it out about 3 mm/$^1/_8$ inch thick. Set aside and leave to cool completely.

4 Use a sharp knife to cut the mixture into 8 strips, each 4 cm/1$^1/_2$ inches wide, then cut each strip in half so it is 15 cm/6 inches long. Use a round-bladed knife to lift up the strips, then roll them up like a Swiss roll. Transfer the rolls to a serving platter and chill until required.

5 Just before serving, heat the oil in a saucepan or frying pan over a medium heat. Add the mustard and sesame seeds and fry, stirring constantly, until they start to pop. Immediately remove the pan from the heat, add the chilli and stir it around in the residual heat for 30 seconds longer, then pour the oil and spices over the rolls. Sprinkle with the coriander and serve.

*cook's tip

If you don't have a square 30-cm/12-inch baking tray, simply grease the area of those measurements on a clean work surface and spread the mixture out until it is 3 mm/$^1/_8$ inch thick.

spicy prawns with cucumber
masala jhinga aur kakdi

High-tech computer industries have clustered in Bangalore, giving this ancient and traditional town a real twenty-first century feel. Along with the wealth have come new-style restaurants with young chefs giving a twist to traditional recipes, such as this dry, crunchy version of Prawn Pooris (for a traditional recipe, see page 185).

SERVES 4–6

2 tomatoes

$^1/_4$ tsp ground coriander

$^1/_4$ tsp ground cumin

$^1/_4$ tsp Garam Masala (see page 251)

1 onion, very finely chopped

200 g/7 oz cucumber, deseeded and finely diced*

250 g/9 oz small cooked, peeled prawns,
  defrosted if frozen

3 tbsp finely chopped fresh coriander

salt

6–8 Pooris (see page 240), to serve

lemon wedges, to serve

1 Bring a saucepan of water to the boil. Cut a small cross in the top of each tomato, then drop it in the boiling water for about 1 minute. Remove the tomatoes from the hot water and immediately plunge into ice-cold water. Peel the tomatoes, then cut them in half, scoop out the seeds and very finely dice the flesh.

2 Put the coriander, cumin and garam masala in a dry frying pan over a medium-high heat and stir for 15 seconds. Add the onion and continue stirring constantly for 2 minutes: the mixture will be very dry.

3 Add the tomatoes and cucumber to the pan and stir for 2 minutes. Add the prawns and stir for a further 2 minutes just to warm them through. Stir in the coriander and salt to taste.

4 Serve hot or at room temperature with the pooris and lemon wedges for squeezing over.

*cook's tip
For a colourful, refreshing version to be served chilled, replace the cucumber with finely diced mango.

This beautifully decorative architectural style is typical of India's many grand palaces and temples

prawn and pineapple tikka 51
jhinga aur annanas tikka

Not long ago, Kerala was a sleepy southern Indian backwater, but now it's a hot tourist destination. Along with its changed status have come boutique hotels, where young chefs make their mark with new-wave flavour combinations, such as this stylish starter. For parties, this looks attractive served on glossy banana leaves.

MAKES 4

1 tsp cumin seeds

1 tsp coriander seeds

1/2 tsp fennel seeds

1/2 tsp yellow mustard seeds

1/4 tsp fenugreek seeds

1/4 tsp nigella seeds

pinch of chilli powder

salt

2 tbsp lemon or pineapple juice

12 raw tiger prawns, peeled, deveined and
   tails left intact*

12 bite-sized wedges of fresh or well-drained
   canned pineapple

chopped fresh coriander, to garnish

Coconut Sambal (see page 247), to serve

1 If you are using long, wooden skewers for this rather than metal ones, place 4 skewers upright in a tall glass of water to soak for 20 minutes so they do not burn under the grill.

2 Dry-roast the cumin, coriander, fennel, mustard, fenugreek and nigella seeds in a hot frying pan over a high heat, stirring them around constantly, until you can smell the aroma of the spices. Immediately tip the spices out of the pan so they do not burn.

3 Put the spices in a spice grinder or pestle and mortar, add the chilli powder and salt and grind to a fine powder. Transfer to a non-metallic bowl and stir in the lemon or pineapple juice.

4 Add the prawns to the bowl and stir them around so they are well coated, then set aside to marinate for 10 minutes. Meanwhile, preheat the grill to high.

5 Thread 3 prawns and 3 pineapple wedges alternately onto each wooden or metal skewer. Grill about 10 cm/4 inches from the heat for 2 minutes on each side, brushing with any leftover marinade, until the prawns turn pink and are cooked through.

6 Serve the prawns and pineapple wedges off the skewers on a plate with plenty of coriander sprinkled over. Serve the coconut sambal on the side.

*cook's tip

To devein the prawns, remove the shell, hold back side up and use a small, sharp knife to make a slash along the length of the prawn from the back to the front, only cutting halfway through the flesh. Use the point of the knife to pick out the thin, black intestine, then discard.

52 # raita potatoes
aloo ka raita

Raitas are often served as a cool, creamy accompaniment to hot, spicy Indian meals, but this potato and yogurt mixture also doubles as a flavoursome salad when served on its own. To make this more substantial for a light lunch, team the creamy mixture with rice and chapatis.

SERVES 4–6

400 g/14 oz new potatoes, scrubbed

salt

1 tsp coriander seeds

1 tsp fennel seeds

400 ml/14 fl oz natural yogurt

1 fresh green chilli, deseeded and finely chopped

pepper

chopped fresh mint, to garnish

4–8 poppadoms, warmed, to serve*

1 Boil the potatoes in salted water for 10–12 minutes until tender when pierced with a fork. Drain and rinse with cold water to cool, then shake dry. When cool enough to handle, finely chop the potatoes with or without peeling them.

2 Meanwhile, dry-roast the coriander and fennel seeds in a hot frying pan over a high heat, stirring them around constantly, until you can smell the aromas. Immediately tip the spices out of the pan so they do not burn.

3 Put the spices in a spice grinder or pestle and mortar and grind to a fine powder.

4 Beat the yogurt in a bowl until it is smooth, then stir in the ground spices, chilli and salt and pepper to taste. Add the potato chunks and stir together without breaking up the potatoes. Cover the bowl with clingfilm and chill for at least 30 minutes.

5 When ready to serve, give the potatoes and yogurt a quick stir, then add lots of chopped fresh mint. Serve with warm poppadoms.

*cook's tip

To fry poppadoms, heat about 1 cm/¹⁄₂ inch vegetable or groundnut oil in a kadhai, wok or large frying pan. Add each poppadom and fry for a few seconds until it expands, turns pale golden brown and small bubbles appear all over the surface. Use tongs to remove from the pan and drain on crumpled kitchen paper. Alternatively, preheat the grill to its highest setting. Brush each poppadom with a little vegetable or groundnut oil and grill for a few seconds on each side.

Intricate stone carvings are often used to depict Indian gods and stories

This is a quick version of the traditional tikka recipe (for a more authentic tandoori recipe try the Tandoori Chicken on page 156). It uses boneless chicken thighs and captures the flavours of Indian cooking without resorting to a jar of sauce. The word 'tikka' means that the dish is made from pieces of chicken or meat rather than a whole bird.

SERVES 4

4 skinless, boneless chicken thighs, cut into strips*

for the tikka paste

150 ml/5 fl oz natural yogurt

2 tbsp lemon juice

1 tbsp Garlic and Ginger Paste (see page 27)

1 tbsp tomato purée

2 tsp Garam Masala (see page 251)

seeds from 2 black cardamom pods

¹/₂ tsp ground cumin

¹/₂ tsp ground coriander

1 tsp paprika

¹/₂ tsp chilli powder

salt

to serve

shredded iceberg lettuce

lemon wedges

chicken tikka 55
murgh tikka

1 To make the tikka paste, mix the yogurt, lemon juice, garlic and ginger paste, tomato purée, garam masala, cardamom seeds, cumin, coriander, paprika, chilli powder and salt, to taste, together in a non-metallic bowl. Add the chicken pieces and stir them around so they are coated. Leave the mixture to marinate for 30 minutes at room temperature, or cover and chill for up to 24 hours.

2 Meanwhile, if you are using long, wooden skewers for this rather than metal ones, place 4 skewers upright in a tall glass of water to soak for 20 minutes so they do not burn under the grill.

3 Preheat an oiled grill to a medium-high setting. If you have refrigerated the chicken, remove it from the refrigerator 15 minutes before grilling. Thread the chicken pieces onto 4 wooden or metal skewers.

4 Grill the chicken for 12–15 minutes, turning over once or twice and basting with any remaining marinade, until it is lightly charred and the juices run clear when pieced with a fork. Serve on the shredded lettuce with lemon wedges for squeezing over. Naans and chutneys make this into a filling first course.

*cook's tip
You can also use the paste with skinless, boneless chicken breasts or lamb fillet. Marinate the lamb for as long as possible, preferably overnight.

Overleaf *A general store, selling just about everything you could want, in Goa*

plantain chips
kele ke chips

What could be simpler? These fried plantain chips from Kerala are very moreish so fry plenty. The bananas that grow abundantly in southern India are the small green ones that resemble plantains in the West, and you will find them in Indian or Caribbean food markets. They are delicious served straight from the pan with a chutney for dipping.

SERVES 4

4 ripe plantains*

1 tsp mild, medium or hot curry powder, to taste

vegetable or groundnut oil, for deep-frying

grated fresh coconut (optional)

1 Peel the plantains, then cut crossways into 3-mm/⅛-inch slices. Put the slices in a bowl, sprinkle over the curry powder and use your hands to lightly toss together.

2 Heat enough oil for deep-frying in a kadhai, wok, deep-fat fryer or large heavy-based saucepan to 180°C/350°F, or until a cube of bread browns in 30 seconds. Add as many plantain slices as will fit in the pan without overcrowding and fry for 2 minutes, or until golden.

3 Remove the plantain chips from the pan with a slotted spoon and drain well on crumpled kitchen paper. If you have a fresh coconut, use a fine grater to grate fresh flakes over the chips while they are still hot. Serve at once.

**cook's tip*
Ordinary yellow-skinned bananas can also be used in this recipe, but the frying will take a little less time.

An old man in traditional Indian dress plays a wooden instrument similar to a flute

paneer tikka
paneer tikka

For India's millions of vegetarians, paneer, this firm, white cheese, is the main source of dietary protein. It has very little taste on its own, which is why it is paired here with a hot, spicy tikka paste. The contrasting flavours produce a medium-hot dish that calls out for a cool beer.

SERVES 4

350 g/12 oz Paneer (see page 252), cut into 16 cubes

melted Ghee (see page 253), or vegetable or groundnut
    oil, for brushing

1 tsp Garam Masala (see page 251)

fresh coriander leaves, to garnish

for the tikka paste*

10 black peppercorns

6 cloves

seeds from 4 green cardamom pods

1 tsp cumin seeds

1 tsp coriander seeds

$^{1}/_{2}$ tsp poppy seeds

$^{1}/_{2}$ tsp chilli powder

$^{1}/_{2}$ tsp ground turmeric

2 tbsp Garlic and Ginger Paste (see page 27)

1 wedge of onion, chopped

150 ml/5 fl oz natural yogurt

$^{1}/_{2}$ tbsp tomato purée

1 tbsp besan or gram flour

1 tbsp vegetable or groundnut oil

1 To make the tikka paste, dry-roast the peppercorns, cloves, cardamom and the cumin, coriander and poppy seeds in a hot frying pan over a high heat, stirring constantly, until you can smell the aroma. Immediately tip the spices out of the pan so they don't burn.

2 Put the spices in a spice grinder or pestle and mortar. Add the chilli powder and turmeric and grind the spices to a fine powder. Add the garlic and ginger paste and onion and continue grinding until a paste forms. Transfer to a large bowl and stir in the yogurt, tomato purée, besan flour and oil.

3 Add the paneer to the bowl and use your hands to coat the cubes in the tikka paste, taking care not to break up the pieces of cheese. Set aside for 30 minutes to marinate at room temperature, or cover the bowl with clingfilm and chill for up to 24 hours.

4 Meanwhile, if you are using long, wooden skewers for this rather than metal ones, place 4 skewers upright in a tall glass of water to soak for 20 minutes so they do not burn under the grill.

5 Preheat the grill to a medium-high setting. If you have refrigerated the cheese remove it from the refrigerator 15 minutes before grilling. Lightly rub the 4 wooden or metal skewers with some oil. Thread the cheese cubes onto the skewers, leaving a little space between each cube.

6 Grill the skewers for 12–15 minutes, turning them over once and basting with any remaining tikka paste, until the cheese is lightly charred on the edges. Brush the hot kebabs with the melted ghee, sprinkle with garam masala and garnish with coriander leaves.

*cook's tips

To save time, replace the individual spices with
2 tablespoons bought tandoori masala, sold
in supermarkets and Indian food shops. Add
it to the garlic and ginger paste in Step 2
and continue with the recipe.

These kebabs are good for a quick snack, but if you want
something more filling for a main course, chop 2 cored
and deseeded red and/or yellow peppers into large
cubes and quickly blanch in boiling water, then rinse in
cold water. Thread the Paneer onto the skewers with
alternating pieces of pepper and button mushrooms.

62

cocktail crab cakes
kekda tikki

Traditionally served as a savoury teatime snack that young children enjoy with their mothers, these lightly spiced potato cakes are shaped into bite-sized portions here to serve with cocktails, a chilled glass of beer or a tall, cooling lassi.

MAKES 14

2 large baking potatoes, about 450 g/1 lb, scrubbed
  and cut in half

$^1/_2$ tsp ground turmeric

3 spring onions, very finely chopped

1 fresh green chilli, deseeded and finely chopped

1-cm/$^1/_2$-inch piece of fresh root ginger, grated

2 tbsp finely chopped fresh coriander leaves and stems

finely grated rind of 1 lemon

juice of 2 lemons

200 g/7 oz canned crabmeat, well-drained and flaked*

salt and pepper

vegetable or groundnut oil, for frying

to serve

lemon or lime wedges

chutney or raita

1 Boil the potatoes in their skins in a large saucepan of lightly salted water until they are tender when poked with a fork. Drain well and peel when cool enough to handle.

2 Put the potato flesh in a large bowl and use a potato masher or fork to mash, but not until completely smooth. Add the turmeric and stir until it is well distributed. Stir in the spring onion, chilli, ginger, coriander, lemon rind and lemon juice, to taste. Add the crabmeat and use your hands to work it into the potato mixture so that it is evenly distributed. Season with salt and pepper to taste.

3 Wet your hands and shape the potato mixture into 14 balls, then flatten each into a patty about 4 cm/1$^1/_2$ inches across and 1 cm/$^1/_2$ inch wide.

4 Heat a thin layer of oil in a kadhai, wok or large frying pan over a medium-high heat. Add as many potato cakes as will fit in a single layer without overcrowding the pan and fry for about 4 minutes until golden and crisp. Continue until all the potato cakes are fried.

5 Serve the potato cakes warm or at room temperature with lemon or lime wedges for squeezing over and a chutney or raita for dipping.

*cook's tip
You can substitute canned salmon or tuna for the crab.

Fishing off the coast of Kochi, southern India

64 # onion and tomato salad
cachumber

*This popular everyday Indian salad is typical of
what is served in many restaurants. Teamed with
Chapatis (see page 236) it makes a light meal on its
own, or is an ideal accompaniment to serve with
Lamb Biryani (see page 126) or any tandoori recipe.
Only make it, however, when you have flavoursome
sun-ripened tomatoes.*

SERVES 4–6

3 tomatoes, deseeded and chopped

1 large onion, finely chopped

**3 tbsp chopped fresh coriander, plus a little extra
  for garnishing**

1–2 fresh green chillies, deseeded and very finely sliced*

2 tbsp lemon juice

1 tsp salt

pinch of sugar

pepper

1 Put the tomatoes, onion, coriander and chillies
in a bowl. Add the lemon juice, salt, sugar and
pepper, to taste, then gently toss all together. Cover
and chill for at least 1 hour.

2 Just before serving, gently toss the salad again.
Add extra lemon juice or salt and pepper to taste.
Spoon into a serving bowl and sprinkle with a little
fresh coriander.

*cook's tip

The searing heat in chillies that can make your mouth
feel as if it is burning comes from a chemical called
capsaicin, which is found in the seeds and veins. By
deseeding a chilli you remove the heat, so the flavour
can be enjoyed. To deseed a chilli, use a small, sharp
knife to make a long slice in the chilli from the stem
end to the tip, then use the point of the knife to scrape
out the seeds and veins.

gujarat carrot salad
gajar nu salat

In Gujarat in northwestern India, where this universally popular salad originated, the local carrots are a vibrant red-orange colour.

SERVES 4–6

450 g/1 lb carrots, peeled

1 tbsp vegetable or groundnut oil

$^1/_2$ tbsp black mustard seeds

$^1/_2$ tbsp cumin seeds

1 fresh green chilli, deseeded and chopped

$^1/_2$ tsp sugar

$^1/_2$ tsp salt

pinch of ground turmeric

1$^1/_2$–2 tbsp lemon juice

1 Grate the carrots on the coarse side of a grater into a bowl, then set aside.

2 Heat the oil in a kadhai, wok or large frying pan over a medium-high heat. Add the mustard and cumin seeds and fry, stirring, until the mustard seeds start popping. Immediately remove the pan from the heat and stir in the chilli, sugar, salt and turmeric. Leave the spices to cool for about 5 minutes.

3 Pour the warm spices and any oil over the carrots and add the lemon juice. Toss together and adjust the seasoning, if necessary, then cover and chill for at least 30 minutes. Give the salad a good toss just before serving.

66
malabar hill crab salad
eguru kosumalli

Mumbai's grandest homes are on Malabar Hill, an oasis well above the noisy hustle and bustle of the city with fantastic views over the bay. For the city's stylish ladies-who-lunch and Bollywood stars, this is typical of the refreshing salads enjoyed on cool palm- and flower-bedecked verandas.

SERVES 4–6

350 g/12 oz fresh cooked white crabmeat

3 spring onions, finely chopped

2 tbsp roughly chopped fresh coriander leaves

2 tbsp roughly chopped fresh mint leaves

salt and pepper

2 mangoes, finely chopped*

fresh coriander sprigs, to garnish

lime wedges, to serve

for the dressing

55 g/2 oz creamed coconut

4 tbsp boiling water

1 fresh red chilli, deseeded and finely chopped

finely grated rind and juice of 1 lime

1 To make the dressing, crumble the creamed coconut into a large heatproof bowl and gradually stir in enough of the boiling water for the coconut to dissolve and form a thick liquid. Stir in the chilli and lime rind and add lime juice to taste. Set aside until completely cool.

2 When the dressing is cool, stir in the crabmeat and spring onions, then cover and chill until required.

3 When you are ready to serve, stir the coriander and mint leaves into the salad. Add extra lime juice, if desired, and season with salt and pepper to taste. Add the mango and toss. Garnish with the coriander sprigs and serve on individual plates, with lime wedges for squeezing over.

*cook's tip

If you've never handled a mango before it can seem difficult to peel and stone because the slippery flesh clings to the flat stone in the centre. Hold the unpeeled mango firmly on the work surface with one hand and use a sharp knife to slice off one side, cutting as close to the stone as possible, then repeat on the other side. Cut a crisscross pattern in the flesh on each half, without cutting through the peel, then hold the flesh upwards and gently bend the peel back, cutting out cubes of mango. Cut the flesh away from the stone in the leftover central piece.

chilli chickpea salad 67
chatpate channe

1 Put the yogurt, red onion and chilli in a bowl and stir together. Stir in the chickpeas and set aside.

2 Heat the oil in a kadhai, wok or large frying pan over a medium-high heat. Add the cumin seeds, mustard seeds and asafoetida and stir for 1–2 minutes until the seeds jump and crackle.

3 Immediately tip the hot seeds into the chickpeas and stir around. Add lemon juice and salt and pepper to taste. The salad is now ready to eat, or it can be covered and chilled for up to a day. Serve sprinkled with the chopped fresh mint.

*cook's tip
You can use dried chickpeas to make this flavoursome salad. Soak 200 g/7 oz dried chickpeas in plenty of water overnight. Drain, then place the chickpeas in a large saucepan with fresh water to cover and bring to the boil. Boil for 10 minutes, skimming the surface as necessary, then reduce the heat and leave the chickpeas to simmer for 1–1½ hours, depending on how old the pulses are (the older they are, the longer they will take to become tender). Do not add any salt until the chickpeas are tender. Drain well and add to the yogurt mixture in Step 1 of the recipe.

For the Punjabi Sikhs, dried chickpeas are a winter staple. Here chickpeas are made into a versatile salad, which can be enjoyed as a light starter or as part of a vegetarian meal with a selection of breads and raitas.

SERVES 4–6

4 tbsp natural yogurt

½ red onion, very finely chopped

½ fresh red chilli, deseeded or not, to taste, and finely sliced

400 g/14 oz canned chickpeas, rinsed and very well drained*

2 tsp vegetable or groundnut oil

2 tsp cumin seeds

2 tsp black mustard seeds

pinch of ground asafoetida

1 tsp lemon juice

salt and pepper

chopped fresh mint, to garnish

68 memsahib's mulligatawny soup
mullagatanni

A taste of the Raj that still appears on restaurant menus throughout India. The name of this filling, spiced soup comes from a corruption of the Tamil 'milagu tannir', which translates as 'pepper water'. Soups have never featured large in Indian cooking, so when the British arrived they adapted the Tamils' Rasam (see page 71) to this.

SERVES 4–6

40 g/1¹/₂ oz Ghee (see page 253) or 3 tbsp vegetable
  or groundnut oil

2 large garlic cloves, crushed

2 carrots, diced

2 celery sticks, chopped

1 large onion, chopped

1 large dessert apple, peeled, cored and chopped

1 tbsp besan or gram or plain flour

1–2 tsp mild, medium or hot curry powder, to taste

2 tsp ready-made curry paste

¹/₂ tsp ground coriander

1.2 litres/2 pints vegetable, lamb or chicken stock

2 large tomatoes, chopped

salt and pepper

55 g/2 oz cooked basmati rice (optional)

85 g/3 oz cooked beef, lamb or skinless
  chicken, diced

chopped fresh coriander, to garnish

1 Melt the ghee or heat the oil in a large saucepan or flameproof casserole over a medium heat. Add the garlic, carrot, celery, onion and apple and fry for 5–8 minutes, stirring, until the onion just starts to brown.

2 Stir in the flour, curry powder, curry paste and coriander and continue frying for a further minute, stirring.

3 Stir in the stock and bring to the boil. Add the tomatoes and season with salt and pepper to taste, then reduce the heat, cover and simmer for 45 minutes, or until the vegetables and apple are very tender.

4 Leave the soup to cool a little, then blend it in a food processor or blender until smooth. Use a wooden spoon to press the soup through a sieve into the rinsed pan, discarding any of the remains of the flavourings in the sieve.

5 Add the rice, if using, and stir in the beef, lamb or chicken. Bring to the boil, then simmer for 5 minutes to heat the meat. Ladle into bowls and sprinkle with the coriander.

This sculpture is one of many in the holy southern town of Hampi, home to over a thousand temples

rasam

rasam

This traditional, light broth from Tamil Nadu is believed to be what the Raj cooks took and adapted into Memsahib's Mulligatawny Soup (see page 68). Leaving the seeds in the chilli when you chop it adds an authentic burst of heat.

SERVES 4–6

1¹/₂ tbsp mustard oil

30 g/1 oz tamarind paste

1.2 litres/2 pints hot water

1 large onion, chopped

4 large garlic cloves, chopped

1 fresh red chilli, chopped

4 large tomatoes, deseeded and chopped

1 tsp ground cumin

1 tbsp tomato purée (optional)

1 tbsp black mustard seeds

salt and pepper

fresh coriander leaves, to garnish

1 Heat 1 tablespoon of the mustard oil in a large saucepan over a high heat until it smokes. Remove the pan from the heat and leave the oil to cool. Meanwhile, put the tamarind paste in a bowl and stir in 200 ml/7 fl oz of the hot water, stirring to dissolve the paste.

2 Grind the onion, garlic and chilli into a paste in a spice blender or pestle and mortar.

3 Return the saucepan with the mustard oil to a medium-high heat. Add the onion paste and fry, stirring, for 2 minutes. Stir in the tomatoes, cumin, tamarind liquid and remaining water.

4 Bring to the boil, then reduce the heat, cover and simmer for 5 minutes. Taste and stir in the tomato purée if the tomatoes do not have enough flavour or colour.

5 Meanwhile, heat the remaining mustard oil in a frying pan. Add the mustard seeds and fry, stirring, for 1–2 minutes until they jump and crackle. Immediately tip the seeds out of the pan on to crumpled kitchen paper to drain, then set aside.

6 Leave the soup to cool a little, then process it in a food processor or blender until smooth. Use a wooden spoon to press the soup through a sieve into the rinsed pan, discarding the tomato seeds and skins remaining in the sieve.

7 Reheat the soup and add salt and pepper to taste. Ladle into bowls and sprinkle with the mustard seeds. Garnish with the coriander and serve*.

*cook's tip
To transform this into a light vegetarian meal, serve it Tamil-style, ladled over rice.

72 turmeric yogurt soup
haldi dahi ka shorba

The zingy, vibrant yellow of this creamy vegetarian soup is the unmistakable hue of turmeric, used to colour many Indian dishes. Grown in the large spice plantations of southern India, turmeric is used both in the kitchen and in the medicine cabinet as an antiseptic.

SERVES 4–6

55 g/2 oz besan or gram flour

1 tsp ground turmeric

¹/₄ tsp chilli powder

¹/₂ tsp salt

400 ml/14 fl oz natural yogurt

30 g/1 oz Ghee (see page 253) or 2 tbsp vegetable
   or groundnut oil

700 ml/1¹/₄ pints water

for the garnish*

10 g/¹/₄ oz Ghee (see page 253) or ¹/₂ tbsp vegetable
   or groundnut oil

³/₄ tsp cumin seeds

¹/₂ tsp black mustard seeds

¹/₂ tsp fenugreek seeds

4–6 fresh red chillies, depending on how many
   you are serving

1 Mix the besan flour, turmeric, chilli powder and salt together in a large bowl. Use a whisk or fork and beat in the yogurt until no lumps remain.

2 Melt the ghee in a kadhai, wok or heavy-based saucepan over a medium-high heat. Mix in the yogurt mixture and then the water, whisking constantly. Bring to the boil, then reduce the heat to very low and simmer, still whisking frequently, for 8 minutes, or until the soup thickens slightly and doesn't have a 'raw' taste any longer. Taste and stir in extra salt, if necessary.

3 In a separate small pan, melt the ghee for the garnish. Add the cumin, mustard and fenugreek seeds and stir around until the seeds start to jump and crackle. Add the chillies, remove the pan from the heat and stir for about 30 seconds, or until the chillies blister (if the chillies are fresh they might burst and 'jump', so stand well back).

4 Ladle the soup into bowls and spoon the fried spices over, including a little of the light brown ghee to serve.

*cook's tip

If you don't want to temper the spices (see pages 76–9) for the garnish, spoon a dollop of Coriander Chutney (see page 245) into each portion instead.

VEGETABLE
DISHES

With the largest vegetarian population in the world, it shouldn't be surprising that meatless cooking in India is unequalled in variety and flavours. Fresh vegetables, fruit, pulses, grains, nuts, seeds and dairy products provide endless nutritionally balanced meals, as well as inspiration for Indian cooks.

The richness of Indian vegetarian cooking has evolved over centuries. Many of India's myriad religious and philosophical beliefs meet in vegetarianism. Although Hinduism only prohibits the consumption of beef, millions of Hindus abstain from eating any meat, and Jains and Buddhists, who abhor killing any living creatures, also eschew meat. The ancient traditions of Ayurveda, which promotes good health through herbal treatments and a vegetarian diet, is a way of life for millions. And, of course, so many Indians are vegetarians because the cost of meat can be prohibitive.

Few similarities exist between the culinary traditions of north and south India, but fine vegetarian cooking is one of them. Wherever one travels in India, there will always be a 'veg' option at mealtimes, and even domestic airlines provide 'veg' and 'non-veg' meal options on all flights, regardless of how brief the journey is.

Indian vegetable markets are colourful displays of fresh produce. The country does not have a lot of refrigerated transportation or an integrated fast road or rail network, so usually the fruit and vegetables for sale are local and seasonal. Growers transport and display their produce in wide, shallow baskets,

Wherever one travels in India, there will always be a 'veg' option at mealtimes

with each filled to the brim with only one ingredient, making it easier for eagle-eyed cooks to search out the best.

Dals are a regular feature of vegetarian meals everywhere in India. Dal is the word used to describe both the split pulses (dried lentils, beans and peas) and the numerous dishes prepared with split and whole pulses. Dals provide the inexpensive backbone of most vegetarian meals and they are an excellent low-fat source of fibre. Also, many of the most popular Indian pulses do not require presoaking or lengthy cooking, an obvious bonus for cooks when most Indians eat dal and rice at least once a day. *Dal roti*, or 'dal and bread', is the subsistence food for millions every day.

Anyone new to dal cooking can find the choice of dals available in an Indian food shop bewildering, not at all aided by the inconsistent labelling. The dals used in the recipes in this book include *chana dal* (split yellow lentils or husked Bengal gram), *masoor dal* (split red lentils), *urad dal chilke* (split black lentils or husked and split Egyptian lentils), *urad dal sabat* (whole black lentils) and *kabuli chana* (whole white chickpeas) and they are all available in supermarkets as well as Indian food shops.

The skill Indian cooks display in transforming otherwise dull-tasting and bland-looking pulses into appealing dishes with exciting flavours and varied texture can only be admired. One technique for flavouring dal is to pour hot oil with fried spices and leaves over the dish just before serving. This

Another unique feature of Indian vegetarian cooking is the use of Paneer

is called a *tarka*, or tempering, and is believed to bring the dish alive.

Another unique feature of Indian vegetarian cooking is the use of Paneer (see page 252), the creamy white pressed cheese. Like tofu from China, Paneer is bland tasting on its own, but absorbs flavours from other ingredients it is cooked with. Try Paneer Tikka (see page 60) or Matar Paneer (see page 100) for two different tastes of this very versatile ingredient.

Gujarat, the westernmost Indian state along the Arabian Sea, has a large Jain population who do not use onion or garlic as flavourings and it is considered the home of refined vegetarian cooking. Try Khandvi (see page 47), thin rolls of pastry with a colourful *tarka* for a less-familiar Indian snack. Kitchri (see page 117), the original rice and lentil dish that Raj cooks transformed into kedgeree is from there, as are the Golden Cauliflower Pakoras (see page 42).

Yet, all regions in India have traditional dishes to satisfy non-meat eaters. Try Spiced Pumpkin and Coconut (see page 88) from Bengal, Sambhar (see page 82) from the sunny south, Aloo Gobi (see page 103) from the north and Tomato-Stuffed Aubergines (see page 94) from Maharashtra.

Dishes in other chapters that are ideal for including in vegetarian meals include Raita Potatoes (see page 52), Rasam (see page 71) and Turmeric Yogurt Soup (see page 72). Also, all the recipes in the Desserts & Drinks and the Accompaniments chapters help create a vegetarian feast that captures the delicious flavours of India. All the recipes in this chapter make a main dish size portion.

Left *With no refrigeration, Indian stall-holders rely on shade to keep their produce cool*

Overleaf *A whole team of men is needed to pull these fishing boats up on to the beach*

82
sambhar
sambhar

This light soup-like lentil curry from Tamil Nadu is probably the most typical dish of southern India. With a large vegetarian population in the region, most people will eat one version or another of this every day, starting with breakfast when it is often served with steamed rice cakes called idlis. *Chapatis (see page 236) are just as suitable.*

SERVES 4–6

250 g/9 oz split red lentils (masoor dal), rinsed

175 g/6 oz new potatoes, scrubbed and finely diced

1 large carrot, finely diced

1 green pepper, cored, deseeded and finely chopped

1 litre/1³/₄ pints water

¹/₄ tsp ground turmeric

¹/₄ tsp ground asafoetida

1 tbsp tamarind paste or Tamarind Chutney
  (see page 249)

salt

for the sambhar masala*

3 dried red chillies, stems removed

2 tbsp coriander seeds

2 tsp cumin seeds

2 tsp black mustard seeds

1 tsp black peppercorns

1 tsp fenugreek seeds

3 cloves

¹/₄ tsp ground turmeric

¹/₂ tsp ground asafoetida

1¹/₂ tsp vegetable or groundnut oil

1¹/₂ tbsp split yellow lentils (chana dal)

1 tbsp desiccated coconut

1¹/₂ tbsp split black lentils (urad dal chilke)

for the garnish

1¹/₂ tbsp vegetable or groundnut oil

12 fresh curry leaves or 1 tbsp dried

2 dried red chillies

1 tsp black mustard seeds

1 Put the red lentils in a bowl with enough water to cover and leave to soak for 30 minutes, changing the water once.

2 To make the sambhar masala heat a kadhai, wok or large frying pan over a medium-high heat. Add the chillies, coriander, cumin and mustard seeds, peppercorns, fenugreek seeds and cloves and dry-roast, stirring constantly, until the mustard seeds start to jump, you can smell the aromas and the seeds darken in colour, but do not burn. Stir in the turmeric and asafoetida, then immediately tip the spices into a bowl.

3 Return the pan to the heat. Add the oil and heat, then stir in the split yellow lentils, coconut and split black lentils and fry for about 1 minute until they darken in colour. Tip them out of the pan and add to the other spices.

4 Leave the spice mixture to cool completely, then place in a spice grinder or pestle and mortar and grind to a fine powder.

5 Drain the lentils. Put them in a kadhai, wok or large frying pan with the potato, carrot and pepper and pour over the water. Bring to the boil, skimming the surface as necessary. Reduce the heat to the lowest setting, stir in the turmeric and asafoetida and half cover the pan. Simmer, stirring occasionally, for 15–20 minutes until the vegetables and lentils are tender, but the lentils aren't falling apart.

6 Stir in the tamarind paste and 2 teaspoons of the sambhar masala. Taste and add extra masala and salt to taste. Continue simmering slowly while making the garnish.

7 To make the garnish, heat the oil in a large pan over a high heat. Add the curry leaves, chillies and mustard seeds and stir around quickly, standing back because they will splutter. Transfer the lentils to a serving dish and pour the hot oil and spices over.

*cook's tip

Unlike garam masala, which is the main flavouring mixture of northern dishes and is made from 'hot' spices, sambhar masala is made from what are considered the 'cool' spices, to temper the heat of southern India. It is impractical to make this in small quantities, so store the leftover masala in a sealed jar for up to 4 months, and use to flavour and thicken vegetable and lentil stews. If you don't want to go to the bother of making your own spice mixture, ready-made sambhar masala is sold in Indian food shops.

84

dosa masala
masala dosa

*The most popular snack in southern India, this is
a filling vegetarian feast. Thin, crisp, ghee-rich
pancakes called Dosas (see page 243) are rolled
around a spicy potato and tamarind mixture, an
instant clue that the dish comes from the south.
Although this might not instantly spring to mind
when Westerners think of 'breakfast', this is often
served to start the day. If you are making the dosas,
don't forget to begin soaking the lentils and rice a
day before, and make the batter long enough in
advance for it to ferment. You can buy a packet of
dosa mix from Indian food shops, but the results
aren't as rich or crisp.*

MAKES 8

3 tbsp mustard oil*

2 tsp black mustard seeds

12 fresh curry leaves or 1 tbsp dried

3 fresh green chillies, deseeded and chopped

1¹/₂ large onions, chopped

¹/₂ tsp ground turmeric

750 g/1 lb 10 oz new potatoes, scrubbed and chopped

salt

450 ml/16 fl oz water

¹/₂–1 tbsp tamarind paste or Tamarind Chutney
  (see page 249)

20 g/³/₄ oz creamed coconut, grated and dissolved
  in 1 tbsp boiling water

chopped fresh coriander

8 Dosas (see page 243), kept warm

selection of chutneys, to serve

1 Heat the mustard oil in a large frying pan or
saucepan with a lid over a high heat until it
smokes. Turn off the heat and leave the mustard
oil to cool completely.

2 Reheat the mustard oil over a medium-high heat.
Add the mustard seeds and stir until they start to
jump. Stir in the curry leaves, chillies and onion and fry,
stirring frequently, for 5–8 minutes until the onion is
soft, but not brown.

3 Stir in the turmeric, then add the potatoes and
a pinch of salt. Pour in the water and bring to the
boil. Reduce the heat to the lowest setting and simmer,
covered, for 12–15 minutes until the potatoes are very
tender and almost falling apart and most of the water
has evaporated. Stir in the tamarind paste and coconut,
add extra salt, if necessary, and stir in the coriander.

4 One side of each dosa will be a smooth golden
brown and the other side will be more mottled.
Put one-eighth of the filling on the mottled side and
roll the dosa around it. Continue until all the dosas
are filled. Serve hot or at room temperature with a
selection of chutneys.

*cook's tip
Vegetable or groundnut oil can replace the mustard oil.
If you do this, however, skip Step 1.

hot tomato raita
tamattar ka raita

This colourful and fragrant curry is similar to a warm raita and it goes exceptionally well with plain basmati rice. The inclusion of several varieties of chillies is an indication that it could have originated around Chennai. The spicy heat of the dish will be determined by whether or not the green chillies are deseeded. The more seeds they contain, the hotter the dish will be.

SERVES 4–6

2 tbsp vegetable or groundnut oil

1 tsp mustard seeds

200 g/7 oz shallots, finely sliced

1 tbsp Garlic and Ginger Paste (see page 27)

12 fresh curry leaves or 1 tbsp dried

2 dried red chillies

2 fresh green chillies, deseeded or not, to taste, and chopped

$^1/_2$ tsp ground coriander

$^1/_2$ tsp ground turmeric

8 large, firm ripe tomatoes, about 600 g/1 lb 5 oz, chopped

1$^1/_2$ tbsp tomato purée

300 ml/10 fl oz natural yogurt*

salt

chopped fresh mint, reserving sprig to garnish

1 Heat the oil in a kadhai, wok or large frying pan over a medium-high heat. Add the mustard seeds and stir them around until they start to jump and crackle.

2 Stir in the shallots and garlic and ginger paste and stir for about 5 minutes until the shallots are golden.

3 Add the curry leaves, dried chillies, green chilli, coriander and turmeric, reduce the heat and stir for 30 seconds.

4 Add the tomatoes and tomato purée to the pan and simmer for about 5 minutes, stirring gently, to soften and heat the tomatoes, but not to break them up completely.

5 Remove the pan from the heat and gradually stir in the yogurt, beating well after each addition. Taste and add salt if necessary. Cover the pan and leave to stand for 2–3 minutes, then stir gently. Sprinkle with the fresh mint.

*cook's tip

If you taste various brands of natural yogurt, they will differ in their sourness. If you find this dish too sour, stir in jaggery, an Indian sugar, or light brown sugar.

spiced balti cabbage
bhuni pattagobhi

A quick stir-fry dish that has grown out of the tradition of Balti cooking.

SERVES 4

2 tbsp vegetable or groundnut oil

$^1/_2$ tbsp cumin seeds

2 large garlic cloves, crushed

1 large onion, thinly sliced

600 g/1 lb 5 oz Savoy cabbage, cored and thinly sliced

150 ml/5 fl oz Balti Sauce (see page 155)

$^1/_4$ tsp Garam Masala (see page 251)

salt

chopped fresh coriander, to garnish

1 Heat the oil in a kadhai, wok or large frying pan over a medium-high heat. Add the cumin seeds and stir for about 80 seconds until they start to brown.

2 Immediately stir in the garlic and onion and fry, stirring frequently, for 5–8 minutes until golden.

3 Add the cabbage* to the pan and stir for 2 minutes, or until it starts to wilt. Stir in the balti sauce and bring to the boil, stirring. Reduce the heat a little and simmer for 3–5 minutes until the cabbage is tender.

4 Stir in the garam masala and add salt to taste. Sprinkle with the fresh coriander.

*cook's tip

To make this into a more substantial, filling dish, add 400 g/14 oz drained and rinsed canned chickpeas with the cabbage in Step 3.

88

spiced pumpkin and coconut
kaddu aur nariyal ki sabzi

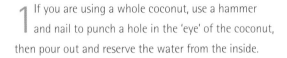

SERVES 4–6

¹/₂ fresh coconut, about 125 g/4¹/₂ oz of flesh*

1 fresh green chilli, deseeded and chopped

1¹/₂ tsp sugar

1 tsp ground coriander

³/₄ tsp ground cumin

¹/₄ tsp chilli powder

2 bay leaves

30 g/1 oz Ghee (see page 253) or 2 tbsp vegetable
   or groundnut oil

600 g/1 lb 5 oz pumpkin, peeled, deseeded
   and coarsely grated

1 tsp Garam Masala (see page 251)

1 If you are using a whole coconut, use a hammer
and nail to punch a hole in the 'eye' of the coconut,
then pour out and reserve the water from the inside.

2 Measure the coconut water and add water, if
necessary, to make 250 ml/9 fl oz. Add the chilli,
sugar, coriander, cumin, chilli powder and bay leaves
to the coconut water and set aside.

3 Use the hammer to break the coconut in half, then
peel half and grate the flesh on the coarse side of
a grater or whiz in a food processor (save the other half
to use in another recipe, such as the Coconut Sambal
on page 247).

4 Melt the ghee in a kadhai, wok or large frying pan
over a medium heat. Add the pumpkin and stir for
1 minute. Add the grated coconut and continue stirring
until the mixture starts to turn brown.

5 Stir in the coconut water. Increase the heat and
continue stir-frying until only about 4 tablespoons
of liquid are left. Sprinkle with the garam masala and
continue stir-frying until all the liquid has evaporated.

cook's tip

Before you buy a coconut, shake it. If you hear a lot of
liquid slushing around inside, it is fresh. If you can't find
a fresh coconut, use 125 g/4¹/₂ oz desiccated coconut
and stir-fry the pumpkin and coconut in a mixture of
125 g/4¹/₂ oz creamed coconut dissolved in 250 ml/
9 fl oz boiling water.

It isn't only Parsis who enjoy this spicy breakfast, this dish is popular throughout southern India and can be transformed into a tempting snack or lunch by serving it on fried bread.

parsi scrambled eggs
akoori

SERVES 4–6

6–8 eggs

4 tbsp single cream or milk

pinch of ground turmeric

salt and pepper

30 g/1 oz Ghee (see page 253) or 2 tbsp vegetable
   or groundnut oil

6 spring onions, finely chopped

2 fresh green chillies, deseeded and chopped

1-cm/$^1/_2$-inch piece of fresh root ginger,
   very finely chopped

2 tomatoes, deseeded and finely chopped

4 tbsp finely chopped fresh coriander

Parathas (see page 239), to serve

1 Crack the eggs into a small bowl and lightly beat, then mix in the cream, turmeric and salt and pepper to taste.

2 Melt the ghee in a kadhai, wok or large frying pan over a medium-high heat. Add the spring onions, chillies and ginger and stir around for 2–3 minutes until the onion is starting to soften.

3 Add the tomatoes and stir around for 30 seconds. Add the egg mixture and half the coriander and stir until the eggs are lightly set and creamy. Taste and adjust the seasoning, if necessary. Sprinkle with the remaining coriander and serve with the parathas.

90 cauliflower, aubergine and green bean korma
sabzi ka korma

Mild and fragrant, this slow-braised mixed vegetable dish reflects the skilled flavouring of Moghul cooking. The rich, almost velvety cream-based sauce is spiced but doesn't contain chillies, making it a rich treat for anyone who prefers mild dishes.

SERVES 4–6

85 g/3 oz cashew nuts

1¹/₂ tbsp Garlic and Ginger Paste (see page 27)

200 ml/7 fl oz water

55 g/2 oz Ghee (see page 253) or 4 tbsp vegetable
  or groundnut oil

1 large onion, chopped

5 green cardamom pods, lightly crushed*

1 cinnamon stick, broken in half

¹/₄ tsp ground turmeric

250 ml/9 fl oz double cream

140 g/5 oz new potatoes, scrubbed and chopped
  into 1-cm/¹/₂-inch pieces

140 g/5 oz cauliflower florets

¹/₂ tsp Garam Masala (see page 251)

140 g/5 oz aubergine, chopped into chunks

140 g/5 oz green beans, chopped into 1-cm/¹/₂-inch pieces

salt and pepper

chopped fresh mint or coriander, to garnish

1 Heat a large flameproof casserole or frying pan with a tight-fitting lid over a high heat. Add the cashew nuts and stir them around just until they start to brown, then immediately tip them out of the casserole.

2 Put the nuts in a spice blender with the garlic and ginger paste and 1 tablespoon of the water and whiz until a coarse paste forms.

3 Melt half the ghee in the casserole over a medium-high heat. Add the onion and fry for 5–8 minutes until golden brown.

4 Add the nut paste and stir for 5 minutes. Stir in the cardamom pods, cinnamon stick and turmeric.

5 Add the cream and the remaining water and bring to the boil, stirring. Reduce the heat to the lowest level, cover the casserole and simmer for 5 minutes.

6 Add the potatoes, cauliflower and garam masala and simmer, covered, for 5 minutes. Stir in the aubergine and green beans and continue simmering for a further 5 minutes, or until all the vegetables are tender. Check the sauce occasionally to make sure it isn't sticking on the base of the pan, and stir in extra water if needed.

7 Taste and add seasoning, if necessary. Sprinkle with the mint or coriander.

*cook's tip
When you serve this, remember to tell guests that it contains cardamom pods, which have a bitter taste if bitten into.

chickpeas with spiced tomatoes
chhole tamattar

In the Punjab, chickpeas are popular year round, and are often included in Sikh festive meals. Here they are made into a versatile salad that can be enjoyed as a light starter or as part of a vegetarian meal with a selection of breads and raitas.

SERVES 4–6

6 tbsp vegetable or groundnut oil

2 tsp cumin seeds

3 large onions, finely chopped

2 tsp Garlic and Ginger Paste (see page 27)

2 small fresh green chillies, deseeded and thinly sliced

1¹/₂ tsp ground mango (amchoor powder)

1¹/₂ tsp Garam Masala (see page 251)

³/₄ tsp ground asafoetida

¹/₂ tsp ground turmeric

¹/₄–1 tsp chilli powder

3 large, firm tomatoes, about 450 g/1 lb, grated*

800 g/1 lb 12 oz canned chickpeas, rinsed and drained

6 tbsp water

300 g/10¹/₂ oz fresh spinach leaves, rinsed

¹/₂ tsp salt

1 Heat the oil in a kadhai, wok or large frying pan over a medium-high heat. Add the cumin seeds and stir around for 30 seconds or until they brown and crackle, watching carefully because they can burn quickly.

2 Immediately stir in the onions, garlic and ginger paste and chillies and fry, stirring frequently, for 5–8 minutes until the onions are golden.

3 Stir in the ground mango, garam masala, asafoetida, turmeric and chilli powder. Add the tomatoes to the pan, stir them around and continue frying, stirring frequently, until the sauce blends together and starts to brown slightly.

4 Stir in the chickpeas and water and bring to the boil. Reduce the heat to very low and use a wooden spoon or a potato masher to mash about a quarter of the chickpeas, leaving the others whole.

5 Add the spinach to the pan with just the water clinging to the leaves and stir around until it wilts and is cooked. Stir in the salt, then taste and adjust the seasoning, if necessary.

*cook's tip

Grating tomatoes is an ingenious technique for eliminating the tough, curled pieces of tomato skins from a dish without having to go to the trouble of peeling the tomatoes first. Just rub the tomatoes firmly up and down on the coarse side of a standard box grater positioned over a bowl. The pulp will go into the bowl and you will be left with the skin and most of the core in your hand.

94

tomato-stuffed aubergines
bharwan baingan tamattari

From Maharashtra, this is an Indian technique for cooking whole, small aubergines with a thin layer of spicy stuffing between the slices. It is an excellent dish for entertaining because the fiddly work can be done well in advance.

MAKES 4

4 small aubergines, about 13 cm/5 inches long

Ghee (see page 253), vegetable or groundnut oil

for the stuffing

4 firm tomatoes, grated

2 onions, grated

2 fresh red chillies, deseeded or not, to taste,
  and chopped

4 tbsp lemon juice

4 tbsp finely chopped fresh coriander

1 tbsp Garlic and Ginger Paste (see page 27)

1½ tbsp ground coriander

2 tsp ground cumin

1 tsp fennel seeds

1 tsp ground turmeric

1 tsp salt

besan or gram flour (optional)

Overleaf The stunning red buildings of the desert city of Jodhpur in Rajasthan

1 To make the stuffing, mix together the tomato, onion, chillies, lemon juice, fresh coriander, garlic and ginger paste, ground coriander, ground cumin, fennel seeds, turmeric and salt in a non-metallic bowl. The filling should not be stiff, but thick enough that it doesn't slide off the aubergine slices. If the tomatoes are very juicy and have made the filling too runny, gradually stir in about 1 tablespoon besan flour.

2 To prepare the aubergines, work with one at a time. Slit each one into four parallel slices, from top to bottom, without cutting through the stem end, so that the aubergine remains in one piece. Lightly fan the slices apart, then use a small spoon or your fingers to fill, dividing a quarter of the stuffing between the slices and covering each slice to the edges. Carefully layer the slices back into position so the aubergine looks whole again. Continue in the same way with the remaining aubergines*.

3 Choose a flameproof casserole or heavy-based frying pan with a tight-fitting lid that is large enough to hold the aubergines in a single layer. Melt enough ghee to cover the base of the pan with a layer about 5 mm/ ¼ inch deep, then add the aubergines in a single layer.

4 Put the pan over the lowest heat and cover tightly. Leave to cook for 15 minutes, then carefully turn the aubergines over. Re-cover the pan and continue cooking for a further 10–15 minutes, or until the aubergines are tender when you pierce them with a skewer or a knife. Check occasionally while the aubergines are cooking, and if they start to stick to the base of the pan, stir in a couple of tablespoons of water. Serve hot or at room temperature.

*cook's tip

This simple dish looks very attractive fanned on a plate for individual servings. For a buffet or party, however, vertically cut the aubergines into 1-cm/½-inch slices. The slices look as though they are from a layered vegetable terrine, but with much less work.

Punjabi cooks took this recipe with them when they left India after the Partition and now it is an Indian restaurant favourite around the world. For the millions of Hindu vegetarians in northern India, however, it remains a regular and important source of protein. Saag is a Hindi word meaning 'greens', and although this is most commonly made with spinach outside India, in India it might include mustard greens, beetroot greens or whatever is available.

SERVES 4

85 g/3 oz Ghee (see page 253) or 6 tbsp vegetable
  or groundnut oil

350 g/12 oz Paneer (see page 252), cut into
  1-cm/^{1}/$_2$-inch pieces

1^1/$_2$ tbsp Garlic and Ginger Paste (see page 27)

1 fresh green chilli, deseeded or not, to taste,
  and chopped

4 tbsp water

1 onion, finely chopped

600 g/1 lb 5 oz fresh spinach leaves, any thick stems
  removed and rinsed

^{1}/$_4$ tsp salt

^{1}/$_4$ tsp Garam Masala (see page 251)

4 tbsp double cream

lemon wedges, to serve

spinach and paneer
saag paneer

99

1 Melt the ghee in a flameproof casserole or large frying pan with a tight-fitting lid over a medium-high heat. Add as many paneer pieces as will fit in a single layer without overcrowding the casserole and fry for about 5 minutes until golden brown on all sides. Use a slotted spoon to remove the paneer and drain it on crumpled kitchen paper. Continue, adding a little extra ghee, if necessary, until all the paneer is fried.

2 Put the garlic and ginger paste and chilli in a spice grinder or pestle and mortar and grind until a thick paste forms. Add the water and blend again.

3 Reheat the casserole with the ghee. Stir in the onion with the garlic and ginger paste mixture and fry, stirring frequently, for 5–8 minutes until the onion is soft, but not brown.

4 Add the spinach with just the water clinging to the leaves and the salt and stir around until it wilts. Reduce the heat to low, cover the casserole and continue simmering until the spinach is very soft.

5 Stir in the garam masala and cream, then gently return the paneer to the casserole*. Simmer, stirring gently, until the paneer is heated through. Taste and adjust the seasoning, if necessary. Serve with lemon wedges for squeezing over.

cook's tip
For a variation, stir 1 or 2 large deseeded and chopped tomatoes into the spinach with the paneer in Step 5.

matar paneer
mattar paneer

Another popular Indian restaurant dish from Punjabi cooks. The sweetness of the peas contrasts well with the richness of the paneer.

SERVES 4

85 g/3 oz Ghee (see page 253) or 6 tbsp vegetable
  or groundnut oil

350 g/12 oz Paneer (see page 252), cut into
  1-cm/¹/₂-inch pieces*

2 large garlic cloves, chopped

1-cm/¹/₂-inch piece of fresh root ginger, finely chopped

1 large onion, finely sliced

1 tsp ground turmeric

1 tsp Garam Masala (see page 251)

¹/₄–¹/₂ tsp chilli powder

350 g/12 oz frozen peas or 600 g/1 lb 5 oz fresh
  peas, shelled

1 fresh bay leaf

¹/₂ tsp salt

125 ml/4 fl oz water

chopped fresh coriander, to garnish

1 Heat the ghee in a large frying pan or flameproof casserole with a tight-fitting lid over a medium-high heat. Add as many paneer pieces as will fit in a single layer without overcrowding the pan and fry for about 5 minutes until golden brown on all sides. Use a slotted spoon to remove the paneer and drain on crumpled kitchen paper. Continue, adding a little extra ghee, if necessary, until all the paneer is fried.

2 Reheat the pan with the ghee. Stir in the garlic, ginger and onion and fry, stirring frequently, for 5–8 minutes until the onion is soft, but not brown.

3 Stir in the turmeric, garam masala and chilli powder and fry for a further 2 minutes.

4 Add the peas, bay leaf and salt, to taste, to the pan and stir around. Pour in the water and bring to the boil. Reduce the heat to very low, then cover and simmer for 10 minutes, or until the peas are tender.

5 Gently return the paneer to the pan. Simmer, stirring gently, until the paneer is heated through. Taste and adjust the seasoning, if necessary. Sprinkle with coriander.

*cook's tip
If you make the paneer for this dish, save 100 ml/3¹/₂ fl oz of the whey and use it to replace the water in Step 4.

Although many Indian women enjoy western fashion, most prefer to wear traditional Indian dress

aloo gobi
aloo gobi

*There must be as many versions of this popular
north Indian dry dish as there are cooks. This is
an excellent accompaniment to all tandoori recipes.*

SERVES 4–6

55 g/2 oz Ghee (see page 253) or 4 tbsp vegetable
   or groundnut oil

$1/2$ tbsp cumin seeds

1 onion, chopped

4-cm/1$1/2$-inch piece of fresh root ginger, finely chopped

1 fresh green chilli, deseeded and thinly sliced

450 g/1 lb cauliflower, cut into small florets

450 g/1 lb large waxy potatoes, peeled and cut into
   large chunks

$1/2$ tsp ground coriander

$1/2$ tsp Garam Masala (see page 251)

$1/4$ tsp salt

fresh coriander sprigs, to garnish

1 Melt the ghee in a flameproof casserole or large
   frying pan with a tight-fitting lid over a medium-
high heat. Add the cumin seeds and stir around for
about 30 seconds until they crackle and start to brown.

2 Immediately stir in the onion, ginger and chilli and
   stir for 5–8 minutes until the onion is golden.

3 Stir in the cauliflower and potato, followed by the
   coriander, garam masala and salt, to taste, and
continue stirring for about 30 seconds longer*.

4 Cover the pan, reduce the heat to the lowest setting
   and simmer, stirring occasionally, for 20–30 minutes
until the vegetables are tender when pierced with the
point of a knife. Check occasionally that they aren't
sticking to the base of the pan and stir in a little
water, if necessary.

5 Taste and adjust the seasoning, if necessary, and
   sprinkle with the coriander to serve.

*cook's tip
For a more golden-coloured dish, add $1/4$ teaspoon
ground turmeric with the other ground spices in Step 3.

*More than three-quarters of Indian villages
have populations of less than a thousand*

madras potatoes
madrasi aloo

Madras Potatoes ... Bombay Potatoes ... similar potato recipes to this appear on most Indian restaurant menus under a variety of names. Waxy potatoes are the best to use because they hold their shape during the rapid frying, but floury potatoes, such as King Edward, are fine as long as you don't mind a texture that is almost falling apart.

SERVES 4–6

900 g/2 lb new potatoes, scrubbed and
   cut into halves or quarters

salt

40 g/1^1/$_2$ oz Ghee (see page 253) or 3 tbsp vegetable
   or groundnut oil

2 tsp black mustard seeds

1 onion, sliced

4 garlic cloves, very finely chopped

2.5-cm/1-inch piece of fresh root ginger,
   very finely chopped

1 fresh red chilli, deseeded or not, to taste,
   and finely chopped

1 tsp ground cumin

^{1}/$_2$ tsp ground coriander

chopped fresh coriander, to garnish

lemon wedges, to serve

1 Put the potatoes in a large saucepan of salted boiling water over a high heat and bring to the boil, then boil for 5–8 minutes, or until tender when pierced with the point of a knife. Drain well, then set aside to cool.

2 Melt the ghee in a kadhai, wok or large frying pan over a medium-high heat. Add the mustard seeds and stir them around for about 1 minute until they start to crackle and jump.

3 Mix in the onion and fry, stirring frequently, for 5 minutes, then stir in the garlic, ginger and chilli and continue frying until the onion is golden.

4 Add the cumin and coriander and stir around until well blended.

5 Add the potatoes and stir until they are hot and coated with spices. Add extra salt, if necessary. Sprinkle with the coriander and serve with the lemon wedges*.

*cook's tip

Served at room temperature these make a good *chaat*, or snack, to serve with an ice-cold beer or a Salt Lassi (see page 212). Just serve with cocktail sticks for picking up.

106

okra bhaji
bhindi ki sabzi

Okra, called 'ladies' fingers' or bhindi *in India, is one of those ingredients that people either devour or shun, usually because the cut pods are cooked in liquid to produce a slimy texture. This quick northern Indian method of frying the crisp green pods eliminates that problem.*

SERVES 4

40 g/1¹/₂ oz Ghee (see page 253) or 3 tbsp vegetable
  or groundnut oil
1 onion, thinly sliced
500 g/1 lb 2 oz okra, stem ends trimmed off
1 or 2 fresh green chillies, deseeded or not,
  to taste, and sliced
2 tsp ground cumin
salt and pepper
¹/₄ tsp Garam Masala (see page 251)
lemon wedges, to serve

1 Melt the ghee in a kadhai, wok or large frying pan over a medium-high heat. Add the onion and fry, stirring frequently, for 2 minutes.

2 Add the okra, green chillies, cumin and salt and pepper, to taste, and continue frying, stirring, for 5 minutes.

3 Sprinkle with the garam masala and continue stirring about 2 minutes longer until the okra are tender, but still crisp*. Serve with lemon wedges.

*cook's tip
For a variation, add 2 deseeded and chopped tomatoes with the okra and chilli or remove the pan from the heat when the okra is tender and slowly stir in 250 ml/9 fl oz natural yogurt, a little at a time, beating constantly.

chilli-yogurt mushrooms
mushroom dahiwale

Another Indian restaurant favourite that is quick and easy to make at home. If you think of mushrooms as bland and uninteresting, think again. The recipe uses chestnut mushrooms, but button mushrooms can be used instead.

SERVES 4–6

55 g/2 oz Ghee (see page 253) or 4 tbsp vegetable
  or groundnut oil

2 large onions, chopped

4 large garlic cloves, crushed

400 g/14 oz canned chopped tomatoes

1 tsp ground turmeric

1 tsp Garam Masala (see page 251)

¹/₂ tsp chilli powder

750 g/1 lb 10 oz chestnut mushrooms, thickly sliced

pinch of sugar

salt

125 ml/4 fl oz natural yogurt

chopped fresh coriander, to garnish

1 Melt the ghee in a kadhai, wok or large frying pan over a medium-high heat. Add the onion and fry, stirring frequently, for 5–8 minutes until golden. Stir in the garlic and fry for a further 2 minutes.

2 Add the tomatoes and their juice and mix around. Stir in the turmeric, garam masala and chilli powder and continue cooking for a further 3 minutes.

3 Add the mushrooms, sugar and salt*, to taste, and fry for about 8 minutes until they have given off their liquid and are soft and tender.

4 Turn off the heat, then stir in the yogurt, a little at a time, beating vigorously to prevent it curdling. Taste and adjust the seasoning, if necessary. Sprinkle with coriander and serve.

cook's tip
Adding the salt with the mushrooms in Step 3 draws out their moisture, giving extra flavour to the juices.

green beans with mustard seeds and coconut

frans bean raiwali

This is a popular southern Indian way to serve beans. It is lightly spiced, so it makes a perfect accompaniment to hot curry dishes.

SERVES 4–6

40 g/1 ¹/₂ oz Ghee (see page 253) or 3 tbsp vegetable
  or groundnut oil

1 tbsp mustard seeds

6 fresh curry leaves or ¹/₂ tbsp dried

1 onion, chopped

¹/₂ tbsp Garlic and Ginger Paste (see page 27)

pinch of ground turmeric

450 g/1 lb green beans, topped and tailed and chopped

55 g/2 oz creamed coconut, grated

250 ml/9 fl oz water

salt and pepper

pinch of chilli powder or paprika, to serve

1 Melt the ghee in a kadhai, wok or large frying pan over a high heat. Add the mustard seeds and stir around for about a minute until they pop. Stir in the curry leaves.

2 Add the onion, garlic and ginger paste* and turmeric and stir for 5 minutes. Add the green beans and stir for 2 minutes.

3 Sprinkle in the creamed coconut, then add the water and bring to the boil, stirring. Reduce the heat to low and simmer, stirring occasionally, for about 4 minutes until the beans are tender, but still have some bite. Taste and adjust the seasoning and sprinkle with a little chilli powder to serve.

*cook's tip

If you like your vegetable dishes with more heat, add 1 chopped fresh green chilli with the garlic and ginger paste in Step 2.

In rural India, animals are important members of the workforce

110 spinach and lentils
palak daal

Vegetarian Indian cooks never seem to run out of ideas for flavourful, quick, everyday meals that combine lentils and other pulses with vegetables. Chana dal are ideal for this simple style of dish because they don't require lengthy soaking or cooking.

SERVES 4

250 g/9 oz split yellow lentils (chana dal), rinsed

1.2 litres/2 pints water*

1 tsp ground coriander

1 tsp ground cumin

$^1/_4$ tsp ground asafoetida

$^1/_2$ tsp ground turmeric

250 g/9 oz fresh spinach leaves, thick stems removed, sliced and rinsed

4 spring onions, chopped

salt

for the garnish

3 tbsp vegetable or groundnut oil

1 tsp mustard seeds

2 fresh green chillies, split lengthways

1-cm/$^1/_2$-inch piece of fresh root ginger, very finely chopped

1 Put the lentils and water in a large saucepan over a high heat. Bring to the boil, reduce the heat to the lowest setting and skim the surface as necessary.

2 When the foam stops rising, stir in the ground coriander, cumin, asafoetida and turmeric. Half-cover and leave the lentils to continue simmering for about 40 minutes, or until they are very tender and only a thin layer of liquid is left on top.

3 Stir the spinach and spring onions into the lentils and continue simmering for a further 5 minutes, stirring frequently, until the spinach is wilted. If the water evaporates before the spinach is cooked, stir in a little extra. Add salt to taste. Transfer the lentils to a serving dish.

4 For the garnish, heat the oil in a small pan over a high heat. Add the mustard seeds, chillies and ginger and stir around until the mustard seeds begin to pop and the chillies sizzle. Pour the oil and spices over the lentils to serve.

*cook's tip

The exact amount of water needed depends primarily on how old the lentils are, but also on the size of the pan. The older the lentils are, the longer simmering they will require to become tender. Unfortunately, there isn't any way to determine the age when you buy lentils, so be prepared to add extra water and increase the cooking time in Step 2. Also, remember, the wider the pan, the quicker the water will evaporate.

Using whole black lentils with their skins still on rather than split lentils adds a gelatinous texture to this rich dal. This dish is time-consuming to prepare, so it is more likely to be prepared in restaurants or for special occasions than on an everyday basis.

black dal 113
maah ki daal

SERVES 4–6

250 g/9 oz whole black lentils (urad dal sabat)

115 g/4 oz dried red kidney beans

4 garlic cloves, cut in half

4 black cardamom pods, lightly crushed

2 bay leaves

1 cinnamon stick

115 g/4 oz butter

1¹/₂ tbsp Garlic and Ginger Paste (see page 27)

2 tbsp tomato purée

¹/₂ tsp chilli powder

pinch of sugar

salt

150 ml/5 fl oz double cream

fresh coriander sprigs, to garnish

1 Put the lentils and kidney beans in separate bowls with plenty of water to cover and leave to soak for at least 3 hours, but ideally overnight.

2 Meanwhile, put the garlic cloves, cardamom pods, bay leaves and cinnamon stick in a piece of muslin and tie together into a bundle.

3 Drain the lentils and kidney beans separately. Put the kidney beans in a kadhai, wok or large saucepan with twice their volume of water and bring to the boil, then boil for 10 minutes and drain well.

4 Return the kidney beans to the pan, add the black lentils and cover with double their volume of water. Add the spice bag and bring to the boil over a high heat, then reduce the heat to low and simmer*, partially covered, for about 3 hours, skimming the surface as necessary, until the pulses are very tender and reduced to a thick paste. Mash the pulses against the side of the pan with a wooden spoon or a potato masher every 15 minutes while they are simmering.

5 When the pulses are almost cooked, remove the spice bag and set aside to cool. Melt the butter in a small pan. Add the garlic and ginger paste and stir around for 1 minute. Stir in the tomato, chilli powder, sugar and salt, to taste, and continue simmering for 2–3 minutes.

6 When the spice bag is cool enough to handle, squeeze all the flavouring juices into the pulses. Stir the butter and spice mixture into the pulses, along with all but 2 tablespoons of the cream. Bring to the boil, then reduce the heat and simmer for 10 minutes, stirring occasionally.

7 Transfer the dal to a serving dish, then swirl with the remaining cream and sprinkle with the coriander.

*cook's tip
Watch the pulses closely while they are simmering in Step 4, and stir in extra water if it evaporates before the pulses are tender.

114 sweet-and-sour lentils
khatti meethi daal

This is the Bengali style of preparing yellow lentils.

SERVES 4

250 g/9 oz split yellow lentils (chana dal)

1.2 litres/2 pints water

2 bay leaves, torn

3 fresh chillies, sliced once, but left whole

$^1/_2$ tsp ground turmeric

$^1/_2$ tsp ground asafoetida

3 tbsp vegetable or groundnut oil

$^1/_2$ onion, finely chopped

2-cm/$^3/_4$-inch piece of fresh root ginger, finely chopped

30 g/1 oz creamed coconut, grated

1 fresh green chilli, deseeded or not, to taste,
  and chopped

1$^1/_2$ tbsp sugar

1$^1/_2$ tbsp tamarind paste or Tamarind
  Chutney (see page 249)

$^1/_2$ tsp Garam Masala (see page 251)

$^1/_4$ tsp ground cumin

$^1/_4$ tsp ground coriander

salt*

to garnish

15 g/$^1/_2$ oz Ghee (see page 253), melted, or
  1 tbsp vegetable or groundnut oil

1 tsp Garam Masala (see page 251)

chopped fresh coriander

1 Put the lentils and water in a large saucepan with a lid over a high heat and bring to the boil, skimming the surface as necessary. When the foam stops rising, stir in the bay leaves, chillies, turmeric and asafoetida. Half-cover the pan and leave the lentils to continue simmering for about 40 minutes, or until they are very tender, but not reduced to a mush, and all the liquid has been absorbed.

2 When the lentils are almost tender, heat the oil in a kadhai, wok or large frying pan over a medium-high heat. Add the onion and ginger and fry, stirring frequently, for 5–8 minutes.

3 Stir in the coconut, green chilli, sugar, tamarind paste, garam masala, ground cumin and ground coriander and stir around for about 1 minute.

4 When the lentils are tender, add them, the bay leaves, chillies and any liquid left in the saucepan to the spice mixture and stir around to blend together. Taste and add salt, if necessary, and extra sugar and tamarind, if desired.

5 Transfer the lentils to a serving dish and drizzle the hot ghee over the top. Sprinkle with garam masala and coriander.

*cook's tip

Neither lentils nor any pulses should be seasoned with salt until after they are tender. If salt is added too soon, it will draw out any moisture so the lentils remain too dehydrated to digest easily.

kitchri
khichdee

This recipe makes a light meal on its own, served with hot bread and a raita, but it is also excellent to team with other vegetarian dishes. This is the traditional Indian dish that British cooks of the Raj adapted into kedgeree.

SERVES 4–6

225 g/8 oz basmati rice

30 g/1 oz Ghee (see page 253) or 2 tbsp vegetable
   or groundnut oil

1 large onion, finely chopped

250 g/9 oz split red lentils (masoor dal), rinsed*

2 tsp Garam Masala (see page 251)

1¹/₂ tsp salt

pinch of ground asafoetida

850 ml/1¹/₂ pints water

2 tbsp chopped fresh coriander

to serve

Chapatis (see page 236)

Raita (see page 244)

1 Rinse the basmati rice in several changes of water until the water runs clear, then leave to soak for 30 minutes. Drain and set aside until ready to cook.

2 Melt the ghee in a flameproof casserole or large saucepan with a tight-fitting lid over a medium-high heat. Add the onion and fry for 5–8 minutes, stirring frequently, until golden, but not brown.

3 Stir in the rice and lentils along with the garam masala, salt and asafoetida, and stir for 2 minutes. Pour in the water and bring to the boil, stirring.

4 Reduce the heat to as low as possible and cover the pan tightly. Simmer without lifting the lid for 20 minutes until the grains are tender and the liquid is absorbed. Re-cover the pan, turn off the heat and leave to stand for 5 minutes.

5 Use 2 forks to mix in the coriander and adjust the seasoning, if necessary. Serve with chapatis and raita.

cook's tip

It's useful to keep a supply of lentils in the cupboard as, unlike other pulses, they do not need lengthy soaking before cooking. When you buy them in the supermarket, they will be ready to use straight from the packet, but if you buy them loose in Asian or health food shops, pick them over and rinse them to remove any grit. Lentils that have been on the shelf for a long time might take longer to cook.

MEAT & POULTRY DISHES

Almost any meat dish other than those served in a hotel in India can give some indication of the host's religious background. Meat-eating Hindus and Sikhs abstain from ever eating beef, and Muslims and kosher Jews do not touch pork. Christians and Parsis, on the other hand, eat all forms of meat, restricted only by expense.

Against this background of intertwined religion and food, the humble goat has emerged as the most popular red meat eaten in India. One piece of Indian folklore maintains that skilled northern Indian cooks can prepare a different goat dish for each day of the year. The exception is in Kashmir, where sheep graze on the mountains to make meat meltingly tender.

As traditional Indian recipes have been exported to Indian restaurants around the world, goat has been replaced with lamb, which is the meat used for recipes in this book. Chicken, regarded as an everyday meat in many other countries, might be scrawny-looking in India, but it is for the most part free-range and considered a choice treat, especially by Punjabi Hindus who serve it for wedding banquets and other large celebrations.

Meat features more in the daily diet of the northern states of Rajasthan, the Punjab and Kashmir than elsewhere in India, and it is the northern Indian meat dishes that are most recognized outside the country. This is because it was Punjabis who opened the first Indian restaurants abroad and brought with them the rich tradition of Moghul cooking that has thrived since the last great invasion of the sixteenth century.

Tandoori cooking is one of the lasting legacies of the Moghul dynasties

Tandoori cooking is one of the lasting legacies of the Moghul dynasties. The tradition of cooking meat, poultry, fish and to a lesser extent vegetables in a tall, charcoal-heated clay oven called a *tandoor* originated in northeastern Persia, and the technique has remained unchanged in the intervening centuries. Food, which is often first tenderized in a yogurt marinade, is cooked from the dry heat at the bottom and from the reflected heat of the sides. Lamb and chicken kebabs are particularly suited to this method. It is impossible to re-create the authentic flavours of tandoori cooking without a *tandoor* oven, but the Tandoori Chicken (see page 156) and Chicken Tikka (see page 55) recipes give similar results. Coriander Lamb Kebabs (see page 133) is another tandoori-style recipe adapted for domestic ovens.

The Moghul court cooks also brought with them rich recipes, incorporating creamy sauces, spices, sweet fresh and plump dried fruits and tender nuts. Moghul cooking reached its height with the rice and meat biryanis of the Nizam's royal kitchens in Hyderabad. Cooks here were unrivalled in their lavish, refined cooking. Lamb Biryani (see page 126) is a dish for celebrations, if only because it is time-consuming to prepare, but worth the effort for the subtle flavouring, wonderful aromas and tenderness. The golden saffron finish alludes to its regal origins.

To sample other meat and poultry dishes that have evolved from Moghul kitchens, try Butter Chicken (see page 158) and Kashmiri Chicken (see page 162).

Cauliflower, Aubergine and Green Bean Korma (see page 90) is a mild and rich vegetarian dish in the Moghul style.

Parsis, who fled persecutions in Persia centuries ago, are also meat-eaters, and their Persian heritage is reflected in rich and subtly flavoured dishes. Try Lamb Dhansak (see page 138) to sample a thick, smooth sauce made from disintegrating lentils and pumpkin.

Hot and spicy Pork Vindaloo (see page 148) from Goa's Christian community is probably the country's best-known pork recipe. This tongue-tingling dish, generously flavoured with fresh chillies as well as garlic and vinegar, reflects the years of Portuguese rule. Although vindaloos appear on restaurant menus made with beef and lamb, the pork version is authentic.

All meats, including pork, feature in Anglo-Indian cooks' repertoires. Anglo-Indian food is a hybrid of the bland food of the British Raj and traditional spiced Indian dishes, very much like the Indian food served in restaurants a decade or so ago. Try the Anglo-Indian Railroad Pork and Vegetables (see page 147) and the traditional Kheema Matar (see page 151) to see how the styles differ. Both are made with minced meat and are ideal for family meals, but completely different.

Authentic Indian meat and poultry recipes often require lengthy cooking to tenderize the meat to the point where it can be pulled into bite-sized pieces with fingers, and often meat is not taken off the bones during cooking, adding extra flavour. The recipes in this book, however, require less cooking because they are intended to be eaten with knives and forks, and many recipes use boneless meat for convenience of cooking and preparation.

Overleaf *Palm trees are an important source of food in the south, providing oil, coconut meat and milk*

126 lamb biryani
gosht biryani

From the Moghul courts of Hyderabad, this elaborate combination of rice and meat remains the Indian dish of choice for non-vegetarian weddings and celebrations.

SERVES 6–8

40 g/1¹⁄₂ oz Ghee (see page 253) or 3 tbsp vegetable
  or groundnut oil

1 kg/2 lb 4 oz boneless leg of lamb, trimmed, patted dry
  and cut into 5-cm/2-inch pieces

salt and pepper

1¹⁄₄ large onions, finely chopped

1¹⁄₂ tbsp Garam Masala (see page 251)

¹⁄₂ tsp cumin seeds

1 cinnamon stick, broken in half

2.5-cm/1-inch piece of fresh root ginger, finely chopped

3 large garlic cloves, crushed

¹⁄₂ tsp ground turmeric

¹⁄₂ tsp chilli powder

700 ml/1¹⁄₄ pints chicken stock

30 g/1 oz fresh coriander leaves

500 g/1 lb 2 oz basmati rice

6 tbsp milk

1 tsp saffron threads

150 ml/5 fl oz natural yogurt

to garnish

³⁄₄ large onion, finely sliced

1 tsp salt

4 tbsp vegetable or groundnut oil

100 g/3¹⁄₂ oz sultanas

100 g/3¹⁄₂ oz blanched almonds

3 hard-boiled eggs, halved lengthways

chopped fresh coriander

1 Melt 30 g/1 oz of the ghee in a large flameproof casserole over a medium-high heat. Add the lamb, season well and brown on all sides, then transfer to a plate. Work in batches, if necessary.

2 Wipe out the casserole and melt the remaining ghee over a medium heat. Add the chopped onion and fry, stirring frequently, for 5–8 minutes until soft and golden, but not brown. Stir in the garam masala, cumin seeds and cinnamon and continue frying, stirring, for 2–3 minutes until you can smell the aromas.

3 Return the lamb and all its juices to the casserole. Add the ginger, garlic, turmeric and chilli powder and stir around for 3 minutes, or until you can smell the aromas. Add the chicken stock and coriander and bring to the boil. Reduce the heat to the lowest setting, cover the casserole and leave to simmer for 1¹⁄₂ hours (the lamb should not be completely tender at this point).

4 Meanwhile, prepare the rice, milk and garnish. Rinse the rice in several changes of cold water until the water is clear, then set the rice aside to soak for 20 minutes in plenty of water to cover.

5 To make the saffron milk, heat the milk until it simmers in a small saucepan, crumble in the saffron and set aside to steep.

6 To make the dark onion garnish, put the sliced onion in a bowl, sprinkle with the salt and leave to stand for about 5 minutes to extract the moisture. Use your hands to squeeze out the moisture. Heat half the oil in a frying pan over a high heat. Add the onion and fry, stirring constantly, for 4–6 minutes until golden brown. Immediately tip out of the pan as it will continue to darken as it cools (if you wait until the onion is dark brown before you remove from the pan, it will develop a burnt taste). Set the onion aside*.

7 Wipe out the frying pan and melt the remaining oil in it. Add the sultanas and fry, stirring, for 3–5 minutes until they are golden, then immediately

remove them from the pan with a slotted spoon. Add the almonds to the fat remaining in the pan and stir them around for 2–3 minutes until they turn golden brown, watching carefully because they can burn in seconds.

8 After the rice has soaked, drain it. Bring a large saucepan of water to the boil. Add the rice and cook for 5 minutes (it will not be completely tender at this point). Drain well and set aside.

9 Preheat the oven to 190°C/375°F/Gas Mark 5. Take the lamb off the heat and stir in the yogurt, a little at a time, stirring very fast to prevent it curdling. Adjust the seasoning.

10 Spoon the partially cooked rice over the lamb, mounding it up. Use the handle of a wooden spoon to make a hole in the centre of the rice, moving the spoon around until the hole is about 2.5 cm/1 inch wide. Drizzle the saffron milk over the rice in 'spokes' coming out from the centre.

11 Cover the casserole and bake for 40 minutes. Remove the casserole from the oven and leave to stand for 5 minutes without lifting the lid.

12 Uncover the casserole and sprinkle the raisins and almonds over the top. Add the browned onion slices and hard-boiled eggs and sprinkle with fresh coriander. Serve straight from the casserole.

*cook's tip
A biryani dish like this is time-consuming to prepare, but Steps 1–6 can be done a day in advance.

rogan josh 129
rogan josh

Originally from Kashmir, this fragrant rich dish was quickly adopted by Moghul cooks and has remained a firm favourite in northern India ever since. A Kashmiri natural dye called rattanjog *traditionally provided the characteristic red colour, but chilli powder and tomato purée provide a more readily available, and less expensive, alternative in this recipe.*

SERVES 4

350 ml/12 fl oz natural yogurt

1/2 tsp ground asafoetida dissolved in 2 tbsp water

700 g/1 lb 9 oz boneless leg of lamb, trimmed and cut
   into 5-cm/2-inch cubes

2 tomatoes, deseeded and chopped

1 onion, chopped

30 g/1 oz Ghee (see page 253) or 2 tbsp vegetable
   or groundnut oil

1 1/2 tbsp Garlic and Ginger Paste (see page 27)

2 tbsp tomato purée

2 bay leaves

1 tbsp ground coriander

1/4–1 tsp chilli powder, ideally Kashmiri chilli powder*

1/2 tsp ground turmeric

1 tsp salt

1/2 tsp Garam Masala (see page 251)

1 Put the yogurt in a large bowl and stir in the dissolved asafoetida. Add the lamb and use your hands to rub in all the marinade, then set aside for 30 minutes.

2 Meanwhile, put the tomatoes and onion in a blender and whiz until blended. Melt the ghee in a flameproof casserole or large frying pan with a tight-fitting lid. Add the garlic and ginger paste and stir around until you can smell cooked garlic.

3 Stir in the tomato mixture, tomato purée, bay leaves, coriander, chilli powder and turmeric, reduce the heat to low and simmer, stirring occasionally, for 5–8 minutes.

4 Add the lamb and salt with any leftover marinade and stir around for 2 minutes. Cover, reduce the heat to low and simmer, stirring occasionally, for 30 minutes. The lamb should give off enough moisture to prevent it catching on the base of the pan, but if the sauce looks too dry, stir in a little water.

5 Sprinkle the lamb with the garam masala, re-cover the pan and continue simmering for 15–20 minutes until the lamb is tender when poked with a fork. Adjust the seasoning, if necessary.

*cook's tip
For an authentic flavour, search out the bright-red Kashmiri chilli powder sold at Indian food shops.

130

lamb pasanda
gosht pasanda

A legacy from the glorious days of the Moghul courts, when Indian cooking reached a refined peak. This rich, creamy dish gets its name from the word 'pasanda', which indicates small pieces of boneless meat, in this case tender lamb, flattened as thin as possible.

SERVES 4-6

600 g/1 lb 5 oz boneless lamb shoulder or leg

2 tbsp Garlic and Ginger Paste (see page 27)

55 g/2 oz Ghee (see page 253) or 4 tbsp vegetable
or groundnut oil

3 large onions, chopped

1 fresh green chilli, deseeded and chopped (optional)

2 green cardamom pods, lightly crushed

1 cinnamon stick, broken in half

2 tsp ground coriander

1 tsp ground cumin

1 tsp ground turmeric

250 ml/9 fl oz water

150 ml/5 fl oz double cream

4 tbsp ground almonds

1$^{1}/_{2}$ tsp salt

1 tsp Garam Masala (see page 251)

to garnish

paprika

toasted flaked almonds*

1 Cut the meat into thin slices, then place the slices between clingfilm and bash with a rolling pin or meat mallet to make them even thinner. Put the lamb slices in a bowl, add the garlic and ginger paste and use your hands to rub the paste into lamb. Cover and set aside in a cool place to marinate for 2 hours.

2 Melt the ghee in a flameproof casserole or large frying pan with a tight-fitting lid over a medium-high heat. Add the onion and chilli and fry, stirring frequently, for 5–8 minutes until the onion is golden brown.

3 Stir in the cardamom pods, cinnamon stick, coriander, cumin and turmeric and continue stirring for 2 minutes, or until the spices are aromatic.

4 Add the meat to the pan and fry, stirring occasionally, for about 5 minutes until it is brown on all sides and the fat begins to separate. Stir in the water and bring to the boil, still stirring. Reduce the heat to its lowest setting, cover the pan tightly and simmer for 40 minutes, or until the meat is tender.

5 When the lamb is tender, stir the cream and almonds together in a bowl. Beat in 6 tablespoons of the hot cooking liquid from the pan, then gradually beat this mixture back into the casserole. Stir in the salt and garam masala. Continue to simmer for a further 5 minutes, uncovered, stirring occasionally.

6 Garnish with a sprinkling of paprika and toasted flaked almonds to serve.

*cook's tip

To toast flaked almonds, put them in a dry frying pan over a medium heat and stir constantly until they turn golden brown. Immediately tip them out of the pan because they can burn quickly. Alternatively, toast them in a preheated oven, 180°C/350°F/Gas Mark 4, on a baking sheet for 10–15 minutes until golden.

coriander lamb kebabs

gosht hara kabab

As you walk through any bazaar or market in a northern Indian city, street vendors will cook these fragrant and subtly spiced kebabs to order. They are cooked in a tandoor oven to produce a dry exterior that keeps the centre tender, but using a hot preheated grill or cooking over glowing coals also give good results.

MAKES 4–6 SKEWERS

700 g/1 lb 9 oz minced lamb

1 onion, grated

3 tbsp finely chopped fresh coriander leaves and stems

3 tbsp finely chopped fresh mint

3 tbsp besan or gram flour

1½ tbsp ground almonds

2.5-cm/1-inch piece of fresh root ginger, grated

3 tbsp lemon juice

2 tbsp natural yogurt

2 tsp ground cumin

2 tsp ground coriander

1½ tsp salt

1½ tsp Garam Masala (see page 251)

1 tsp ground cinnamon

pepper, to taste

lemon wedges, to serve

1 Place all the ingredients in a large bowl and use your hands to incorporate everything until the texture is smooth. Cover the bowl with a tea towel and leave to stand for about 45 minutes at room temperature.

2 With wet hands, divide the minced lamb mixture into 24 equal balls*. Working with one ball at a time, mould it around a long, flat metal skewer, shaping it into a cylinder shape. Continue until all the mixture has been used and you have filled 4 or 6 skewers.

3 Preheat the grill to its highest setting or light barbecue coals and leave to burn until they turn grey. Lightly brush the grill rack or barbecue grid with oil. Add the skewers and grill for 5–7 minutes, turning frequently, until the lamb is completely cooked through and not at all pink when you pierce it with the point of a knife. Serve with lemon wedges for squeezing over and a salad.

cook's tip

If you don't want to be bothered shaping the lamb mixture into skewers, form 6 patties. Grill as above, but increase the cooking time to 4 minutes on each side.

134 # sesame lamb chops
champ tilwale

In much of India these chops, with their fragrant crunchy coating, would be made with young goat, but lamb is ideal. The brief marinating period tenderizes the meat, and flattening the meat speeds up the cooking time.

SERVES 4

12 lamb chops, such as best end of neck or middle neck
1¹/₂ tbsp sesame seeds*
pepper
lime wedges, to serve

for the marinade
4 tbsp natural yogurt
2 tbsp grated lemon rind
1¹/₂ tsp ground cumin
1¹/₂ tsp ground coriander
¹/₄ tsp chilli powder
salt

1 To make the marinade, put the yogurt, lemon rind, cumin, coriander, chilli powder and salt, to taste, in a large bowl and stir together.

2 Use a sharp knife to trim any fat from the edge of the lamb chops and scrape the meat off the long piece of bone. Using a rolling pin or the end of a large chef's knife, pound each chop until it is about 5 mm/¹/₄ inch thick.

3 Add the chops to the bowl and use your hands to stir around until they are coated in the marinade. Leave to marinate for 20 minutes at room temperature, or cover the bowl and refrigerate for up to 4 hours.

4 If the chops have been chilled, remove them from the refrigerator 20 minutes before grilling. Preheat the grill to its highest setting and lightly grease the grill rack.

5 Arrange the chops on the grill rack in a single layer, then sprinkle the sesame seeds over each. Grill the chops about 10 cm/4 inches from the heat for about 7 minutes, without turning, for medium.

6 To serve, grind fresh pepper over the chops and serve with lime wedges for squeezing over.

cook's tip
For a variation, omit the sesame seeds and spread a dollop of Coconut Sambal (see page 247) over the top of each chop before grilling.

When you see 'dopiaza' in a recipe title you can be certain it will contain lots of onions and in fact, two types. 'Do' literally means 'two', and 'piaza' means 'onion'. Some recipes will fold in raw onions towards the end of cooking for a crunchy texture, but both sliced and chopped onions are cooked in this very rich version.

lamb dopiaza 137
gosht dopiaza

SERVES 4–6

2 large onions, finely sliced

salt

2 large onions, coarsely chopped

2 tbsp Garlic and Ginger Paste (see page 27)

1/2 tsp ground paprika

2 tbsp chopped fresh coriander

1 tbsp ground coriander

1 tsp ground cumin

1/2 tsp ground asafoetida

70 g/2 1/2 oz Ghee (see page 253) or 5 tbsp vegetable
   or groundnut oil

700 g/1 lb 9 oz boneless shoulder of lamb, trimmed and
   cut into 5-cm/2-inch cubes

4 green cardamom pods

pinch of sugar

1/2 tsp Garam Masala (see page 251)

fresh coriander sprigs, to garnish

1 Put the sliced onions in a bowl, sprinkle with 1 teaspoon salt and leave to stand for about 5 minutes to extract the moisture. Use your hands to squeeze out the moisture.

2 Meanwhile, grind the chopped onions with the garlic and ginger paste, paprika, fresh coriander, ground coriander, cumin and asafoetida in a spice blender or pestle and mortar.

3 Melt 2 tablespoons of the ghee in a flameproof casserole or large frying pan with a tight-fitting lid over a medium-high heat. Add the prepared sliced onions and fry, stirring constantly, for 4–6 minutes until they are golden brown. Immediately tip them out of the pan as they will continue to darken as they cool (if you tip them out when they are brown, they will develop a burnt taste).

4 Melt 2 tablespoons of the remaining ghee in the casserole. Add the lamb and fry to brown on all sides, working in batches if necessary, then remove from the pan.

5 Melt the remaining ghee in the casserole. Add the onion paste and fry, stirring occasionally. Add the cardamom pods and stir around.

6 Return the lamb to the casserole and stir in 1/2 teaspoon salt and the sugar. Reduce the heat to very low, cover the casserole and simmer for 30 minutes*.

7 Uncover the casserole and sprinkle the reserved onion slices and the garam masala over the lamb, re-cover the pan and continue simmering for a further 15 minutes, or until the lamb is tender. Taste and adjust the seasoning, if necessary. Sprinkle with coriander sprigs.

cook's tip
There should be enough moisture in the lamb to prevent the sauce from becoming too thick and catching on the base of the casserole in Step 6, but check occasionally and stir in a little water, if necessary.

lamb dhansak
gosht dhansak

138

For India's numerous Parsis, this rich dish is served for a Sunday family lunch. The lentils and pumpkin dissolve into a velvety-smooth sauce, and all that are needed to complete the meal are rice and naans.

SERVES 4–6

700 g/1 lb 9 oz boneless shoulder of lamb, trimmed
  and cut into 5-cm/2-inch cubes

salt

1 tbsp Garlic and Ginger Paste (see page 27)

5 green cardamom pods

200 g/7 oz yellow lentils (toor dal)

100 g/3¹/₂ oz peeled, deseeded and chopped pumpkin

1 carrot, thinly sliced

1 fresh green chilli, deseeded and chopped

1 tsp fenugreek powder

500 ml/18 fl oz water

1 large onion, thinly sliced

30 g/1 oz Ghee (see page 253) or 2 tbsp vegetable
  or groundnut oil

2 garlic cloves, crushed

chopped fresh coriander or mint, to garnish

for the dhansak masala*

1 tsp Garam Masala (see page 251)

¹/₂ tsp ground coriander

¹/₂ tsp ground cumin

¹/₂ tsp chilli powder

¹/₂ tsp ground turmeric

¹/₄ tsp ground cardamom

¹/₄ tsp ground cloves

1 Put the lamb and 1 teaspoon salt in a large saucepan with enough water to cover and bring to the boil. Reduce the heat and simmer, skimming the surface as necessary until no more foam rises. Stir in the garlic and ginger paste and cardamom pods and continue simmering for a total of 30 minutes.

2 Meanwhile, put the lentils, pumpkin, carrot, chilli and fenugreek powder in a large, heavy-based saucepan and pour over the water. Bring to the boil, stirring occasionally, then reduce the heat and simmer for 20–30 minutes until the lentils and carrot are very tender. Stir in a little extra water if the lentils look as though they will catch on the base of the pan.

3 Leave the lentil mixture to cool slightly, then pour it into a food processor or blender and whiz until a thick, smooth sauce forms.

4 While the lamb and lentils are cooking, put the onion in a bowl, sprinkle with 1 teaspoon salt and leave to stand for about 5 minutes to extract the moisture. Use your hands to squeeze out the moisture.

5 Melt the ghee in a flameproof casserole or large frying pan with a tight-fitting lid over a high heat. Add the onion and fry, stirring constantly, for 2 minutes. Remove one-third of the onion and continue frying the rest for a further 1–2 minutes until golden brown. Use a slotted spoon to immediately remove them from the pan, as they will continue to darken as they cool.

6 Return the one-third of the onion to the pan with the garlic. Stir in all the dhansak masala ingredients and cook for 2 minutes, stirring constantly. Add the cooked lamb and stir for a further 2 minutes. Add the lentil sauce and simmer over a medium heat to warm through, stirring and adding a little extra water, if needed. Adjust the seasoning, if necessary. Sprinkle with the dark onion and serve with coriander sprinkled over.

**cook's tip*

Look in Indian food shops for packets of ready-made dhansak masala. Add 1 tablespoon to the onions in Step 6 and continue with the recipe as above.

In the Punjab, this simple dish would most likely be made with tougher pieces of goat or mutton that require lengthy simmering to become tender, but when made with lamb neck fillets, as here, this makes a quick meal.

lamb with cauliflower
gobhi gosht

141

SERVES 4–6

30 g/1 oz Ghee (see page 253) or 2 tbsp vegetable
  or groundnut oil

1 onion, chopped

¹/₂ tbsp Garlic and Ginger Paste (see page 27)

1 tbsp cumin seeds

2 tsp mild, medium or hot curry paste, to taste

1 head cauliflower, broken into small florets*

400 g/14 oz canned chopped tomatoes

125 ml/4 fl oz vegetable stock or water

salt and pepper

700 g/1 lb 9 oz lamb neck fillet, trimmed and cut into
  5-mm/¹/₄-inch slices

lemon juice, to taste

chopped fresh mint, to garnish

1 Melt the ghee in a kadhai, wok or large frying pan over a medium-high heat. Add the onion and garlic and ginger paste and fry, stirring frequently, for 5–8 minutes until the onion is lightly browned.

2 Add the cumin and curry paste and stir around for about 1 minute. Add the cauliflower and continue stirring for a further minute.

3 Add the tomatoes with their juice, the stock and salt and pepper to taste. Bring to the boil, then reduce the heat and simmer for 10 minutes, stirring occasionally, until the sauce is reduced and the tomatoes break down.

4 Add the lamb and continue simmering, stirring occasionally, for 10 minutes, or until it is tender and just pink in the centre. Add lemon juice to taste and adjust the seasoning, if necessary. Serve garnished with a generous amount of mint.

*cook's tip
For a variation, substitute 1-cm/¹/₂-inch chunks of carrots or broccoli florets for the cauliflower. The broccoli, however, will only require about 5 minutes cooking in Step 3.

India has a high birth-rate and everywhere you go, children gather to welcome you

142 lamb shanks marathani
ghati gosht

From Mumbai, this dish is bursting with lots of flavours that reflect the city's vibrancy and diversity. It's not for nothing that the port city is known as 'The Gateway to India', as traders from all corners of the globe have always sold their wares here. 'Marathani' in a recipe title indicates that a dish comes from the state of Maharashtra, of which Mumbai is the capital.

SERVES 4

55 g/2 oz Ghee (see page 253) or 4 tbsp vegetable
   or groundnut oil

2 large onions, thinly sliced

40 g/1¹/₂ oz cashew nuts

1¹/₂ tbsp Garlic and Ginger Paste (see page 27)

2 fresh green chillies, deseeded and chopped

2 cinnamon sticks, broken in half

¹/₂ tsp chilli powder

¹/₂ tsp ground turmeric

¹/₂ tsp ground coriander

¹/₄ tsp ground mace

3 tbsp natural yogurt

4 lamb shanks

850 ml/1¹/₂ pints water

¹/₂ tsp Garam Masala (see page 251)

salt and pepper

chopped fresh coriander, to garnish

Overleaf *The Ganges River at Varanasi
is one of India's most holy places*

1 Melt half the ghee in a large flameproof casserole over a medium-high heat. Add the onions and fry, stirring frequently, for 5–8 minutes until soft but not coloured. Stir in the cashew nuts and stir around for just 1–2 minutes until they turn light brown.

2 Use a slotted spoon to remove the onions and nuts from the casserole and leave to cool slightly. Transfer both to a food processor or pestle and mortar and grind until a paste forms and the nuts are well ground.

3 Melt the remaining ghee in the casserole. Add the garlic and ginger paste, chillies and cinnamon and stir around for about 1 minute until you can smell the aromas.

4 Stir in the chilli powder, turmeric, coriander and mace. Gradually stir in the yogurt, stirring constantly. Add the lamb shanks and continue stirring for about 5 minutes until the yogurt is absorbed.

5 Stir in the reserved onion and cashew paste. Pour in enough water to cover the lamb shanks, add the garam masala and bring to the boil. Reduce the heat to low, cover the casserole and leave to simmer for 1³/₄–2 hours until the lamb is very tender and almost falling off the bones*.

6 Taste and adjust the seasoning, if necessary. Serve the lamb shanks with the thin sauce spooned over and some chopped coriander.

*cook's tip
The sauce, or 'gravy' as Indians would say, with this dish is very thin. If you prefer a thicker sauce, transfer the lamb shanks to the oven at the end of Step 5. Stir 4 tablespoons of the sauce into 4 tablespoons rice flour to make a smooth paste. Stir the paste into the casserole, bring the sauce to the boil and boil, stirring, for about 10 minutes until reduced and thickened.

railroad pork and vegetables

sabzi gosht

East meets West in the Christian Anglo-Indian kitchens of Kolkata, where the tradition of flavouring British-style dishes with Indian ingredients lives on. This example, not unlike a British savoury pie filling, is an updated version of the railroad curries once served in dining cars.

SERVES 4–6

40 g/1^1/$_2$ oz Ghee (see page 253) or 3 tbsp vegetable
  or groundnut oil

1 large onion, finely chopped

4 green cardamom pods

3 cloves

1 cinnamon stick

1 tbsp Garlic and Ginger Paste (see page 27)

2 tsp Garam Masala (see page 251)

^{1}/$_4$–^{1}/$_2$ tsp chilli powder

^{1}/$_2$ tsp ground asafoetida

2 tsp salt

600 g/1 lb 5 oz lean minced pork*

1 potato, scrubbed and cut into 5 mm/^{1}/$_4$-inch dice

400 g/14 oz canned chopped tomatoes

125 ml/4 fl oz water

1 bay leaf

1 large carrot, coarsely grated

fresh coriander leaves, to garnish

1 Melt the ghee in a flameproof casserole or large frying pan with a tight-fitting lid over a medium heat. Add the onion and continue frying, stirring occasionally, for 5–8 minutes until golden brown. Add the cardamom pods, cloves and cinnamon stick and fry, stirring, for 1 minute, or until you can smell the aromas.

2 Add the garlic and ginger paste, garam masala, chilli powder, asafoetida and salt and stir around for a further minute. Add the pork and fry for 5 minutes, using a wooden spoon to break up the meat, or until no longer pink.

3 Add the potato, tomatoes with their juice, water and bay leaf and bring to the boil, stirring. Reduce the heat to the lowest level, cover tightly and simmer for 15 minutes. Stir in the carrot and simmer for 5 minutes longer, or until the potato and carrot are tender. Taste and adjust the seasoning, if necessary. Garnish with coriander and serve.

cook's tip
Lean minced lamb or beef can be used instead of the pork.

148

pork vindaloo
gosht vindaloo

Not for the faint-hearted! The name 'Vindaloo' comes from the Portuguese words for 'vinegar' and 'garlic', and this traditional Goan dish contains both. The dish's characteristic searing heat, however, comes from the chillies, which the Portuguese introduced along with vinegar when they conquered Goa in 1510. The Portuguese continued to rule this part of western India until it was annexed by India in 1961. One legacy of the Portuguese rule is a large Christian community, which eats pork, unlike many Hindus or Muslims.

SERVES 4–6

4 tbsp mustard oil

2 large onions, finely chopped

6 fresh bay leaves

6 cloves

6 garlic cloves, chopped

3 green cardamom pods, lightly cracked

1–2 small fresh red chillies, chopped

2 tbsp ground cumin

1/2 tsp salt

1/2 tsp ground turmeric

2 tbsp cider vinegar

2 tbsp water

1 tbsp tomato purée

700 g/1 lb 9 oz boneless shoulder of pork, trimmed
   and cut into 5-cm/2-inch cubes

1 Put the mustard oil in a large frying pan or saucepan with a tight-fitting lid over a high heat until it smokes. Turn off the heat and leave the mustard oil to cool completely.

2 Reheat the oil over a medium-high heat. Add the onions and fry, stirring frequently, for 5–8 minutes until soft but not coloured.

3 Add the bay leaves, cloves, garlic, cardamom pods, chillies, cumin, salt, turmeric and 1 tablespoon of the vinegar to the onion and stir around. Stir in the water, then cover the pan and simmer for about 1 minute, or until the water is absorbed and the fat separates.

4 Dissolve the tomato purée in the remaining tablespoon of vinegar, then stir it into the pan. Add the pork and stir around.

5 Add just enough water to cover the pork and bring to the boil. Reduce the heat to its lowest level, cover the pan tightly and simmer for 40–60 minutes until the pork is tender.

6 If too much liquid remains in the pan when the pork is tender, use a slotted spoon to remove the pork from the pan and boil the liquid until it reduces to the required amount. Return the pork to heat through and adjust the seasoning, if necessary.

When the cold winter winds come to northern India, this simple, rustic dish makes a popular family meal.

kheema matar   151
kheema mattar

SERVES 4–6

30 g/1 oz Ghee (see page 253) or 2 tbsp vegetable or groundnut oil

2 tsp cumin seeds

1 large onion, finely chopped

1 tbsp Garlic and Ginger Paste (see page 27)

2 bay leaves

1 tsp mild, medium or hot curry powder, to taste

2 tomatoes, cored, deseeded and chopped

1 tsp ground coriander

$^1/_4$–$^1/_2$ tsp chilli powder

$^1/_4$ tsp ground turmeric

pinch of sugar

$^1/_2$ teaspoon salt

$^1/_2$ teaspoon pepper

500 g/1 lb 2 oz lean minced beef or lamb

250 g/9 oz frozen peas, straight from the freezer

1 Heat the ghee in a flameproof casserole or large frying pan with a tight-fitting lid. Add the cumin seeds and fry, stirring, for 30 seconds, or until they start to crackle.

2 Stir in the onion, garlic and ginger paste, bay leaves and curry powder and continue to stir-fry until the fat separates.

3 Stir in the tomatoes and fry for 1–2 minutes. Stir in the coriander, chilli powder, turmeric, sugar, salt and pepper and stir around for 30 seconds.

4 Add the beef and fry for 5 minutes, using a wooden spoon to break up the meat, or until it is no longer pink. Reduce the heat and simmer, stirring occasionally, for 10 minutes.

5 Add the peas and continue simmering for a further 10–15 minutes until the peas are thawed and hot. If there is too much liquid left in the pan, increase the heat and let it bubble for a few minutes until it reduces.

Many Indians are very interested in politics and photos of political figures are often seen hanging in public places

152 beef madras
madrasi gosht

This spicy curry with a hint of coconut gets its Indian name from the southeastern coastal town of Chennai, formerly known as Madras. The regional specialities are typically flavoured with coconut and lots of chillies, which is why restaurant menus frequently label every hot dish as 'Madras'. Drink chilled beer or a Salt Lassi (see page 212) with this.

SERVES 4–6

1–2 dried red chillies*

2 tsp ground coriander

2 tsp ground turmeric

1 tsp black mustard seeds

$^1/_2$ tsp ground ginger

$^1/_4$ tsp ground pepper

140 g/5 oz creamed coconut, grated and dissolved
  in 300 ml/10 fl oz boiling water

55 g/2 oz Ghee (see page 253) or 4 tbsp vegetable
  or groundnut oil

2 onions, chopped

3 large garlic cloves, chopped

700 g/1 lb 9 oz lean stewing steak, such as chuck,
  trimmed and cut into 5-cm/2-inch cubes

250 ml/9 fl oz beef stock

lemon juice

salt

1 Depending on how hot you want this dish to be, chop the chillies with or without any seeds. The more seeds you include, the hotter the dish will be. Put the chopped chilli and any seeds in a small bowl with the coriander, turmeric, mustard seeds, ginger and pepper and stir in a little of the coconut mixture to make a thin paste.

2 Melt the ghee in a flameproof casserole or large frying pan with a tight-fitting lid over a medium-high heat. Add the onions and garlic and fry for 5–8 minutes, stirring often, until the onion is golden brown. Add the spice paste and stir around for 2 minutes, or until you can smell the aromas.

3 Add the meat and stock and bring to the boil. Reduce the heat to its lowest level, cover tightly and simmer for 90 minutes, or until the beef is tender when you poke it with a fork. Check occasionally that the meat isn't catching on the base of the pan and stir in a little extra water or stock, if necessary.

4 Uncover the pan and stir in the remaining coconut milk with the lemon juice and salt to taste. Bring to the boil, stirring, then reduce the heat again and simmer, still uncovered, until the sauce reduces slightly.

*cook's tip

The dish takes on a different character, but is equally flavoursome, if you omit the chillies altogether and garnish the dish with toasted coconut flakes just before serving.

balti beef
bhuna gosht

Direct from Birmingham, England, this is the Indian/Pakistan version of stir-frying. Immigrants introduced Brummies to this quick style of cooking and now balti restaurants thrive throughout the UK and Europe. It's quick cooking once you've made the balti sauce, but that can be made in advance and refrigerated for several days.

SERVES 4–6

30 g/1 oz Ghee (see page 253) or 2 tbsp vegetable
  or groundnut oil

1 large onion, chopped

2 garlic cloves, crushed

2 large red peppers, cored, deseeded and chopped

600 g/1 lb 5 oz boneless beef for stir-frying, such as
  sirloin, thinly sliced

for the balti sauce

30 g/1 oz Ghee (see page 253) or 2 tbsp vegetable
  or groundnut oil

2 large onions, chopped

1 tbsp Garlic and Ginger Paste (see page 27)

400 g/14 oz canned chopped tomatoes

1 tsp ground paprika

$^1/_2$ tsp ground turmeric

$^1/_2$ tsp ground cumin

$^1/_2$ tsp ground coriander

$^1/_4$ tsp chilli powder

$^1/_4$ tsp ground cardamom

1 bay leaf

salt and pepper

1 To make the balti sauce, melt the ghee in a kadhai, wok or large frying pan over a medium-high heat. Add the onions and garlic and ginger paste and stir-fry for about 5 minutes until the onion is golden brown. Stir in the tomatoes with their juice, then add the paprika, turmeric, cumin, coriander, chilli powder, cardamom, bay leaf and salt and pepper, to taste. Bring to the boil, stirring, then reduce the heat and simmer for 20 minutes, stirring occasionally.

2 Leave the sauce to cool slightly, then remove the bay leaf and pour the mixture into a food processor or blender and whiz to a smooth sauce.

3 Wipe out the kadhai, wok or frying pan and return it to a medium-high heat. Add the ghee and melt. Add the onion and garlic and stir-fry for 5–8 minutes until golden brown. Add the red peppers and continue stir-frying for 2 minutes.

4 Stir in the beef and continue stirring for 2 minutes until it starts to turn brown. Add the balti sauce and bring to the boil. Reduce the heat and simmer for 5 minutes, or until the sauce slightly reduces again and the pepper is tender. Adjust the seasoning, if necessary, and serve in a kadhai.

156 tandoori chicken
tandoori murgh

Don't expect to duplicate this dish exactly as it is
served at your favourite Indian restaurant. That's
impossible to do at home – unless you happen to
have a tandoor oven in the kitchen – but this comes
close, especially if you leave the bird to marinate for
a day before cooking. Indian cooks add the bright
red-orange colour to tandoori dishes with natural
food colourings, such as cochineal. A few drops of
red and yellow food colouring are a more readily
available option for most home cooks, although
it's not necessary. Kashmiri chilli powder will also
enhance the red colour.

*Indian village life is centred around agriculture
and tied to the surrounding villages and cities*

SERVES 4

1 chicken, weighing 1.5 kg/3 lb 5 oz, skinned*

1/2 **lemon**

1 tsp salt

30 g/1 oz Ghee (see page 253), melted

lemon wedges, to serve

for the tandoori masala paste

1 tbsp Garlic and Ginger Paste (see page 27)

1 tbsp ground paprika

1 tsp ground cinnamon

1 tsp ground cumin

1/2 **tsp ground coriander**

1/4 **tsp chilli powder, ideally Kashmiri chilli powder**

pinch ground cloves

1/4 **tsp edible red food colouring (optional)**

few drops of edible yellow food colouring (optional)

200 ml/7 fl oz natural yogurt

1 To make the tandoori masala paste, combine
the garlic and ginger paste, dry spices and food
colouring in a bowl and stir in the yogurt. You can use
the paste now or store it in an airtight container in the
refrigerator for up to 3 days.

2 Use a small knife to make thin cuts over the
chicken. Rub the lemon half all over the chicken,
then rub the salt into the cuts.

3 Put the chicken in a deep bowl, add the paste and
use your hands to rub it all over the bird and into
the cuts. Cover the bowl with clingfilm and refrigerate
for at least 4 hours, but ideally up to 24 hours.

4 When you are ready to cook the chicken, preheat
the oven to 200°C/400°F/Gas Mark 6. Put the
chicken on a rack in a roasting tin, breast-side up, and
dribble with the melted ghee. Roast for 45 minutes,
then quickly remove the bird and roasting tin from the
oven and turn the temperature to its highest setting.

5 Very carefully pour out any fat from the bottom of the roasting tin. Return the chicken to the oven and roast for a further 10–15 minutes until the chicken's juices run clear when you pierce the thigh with a knife and the paste is lightly charred.

6 Leave to stand for 10 minutes, then cut into pieces to serve with lemon wedges for squeezing over.

cook's tip

For a quicker version, use chicken breasts, thighs or drumsticks. Marinate as above, preheat the oven to 230°C/450°F/Gas Mark 8, and roast for about 40 minutes.

butter chicken
murgh makhani

Like Chicken Tikka Masala (see page 161), the quickest way to prepare this popular Sikh dish is to buy ready-cooked tandoori chicken. Otherwise start with the Tandoori Chicken recipe (see page 156). This is a good party dish, with a rich, creamy sauce that you can make as hot as you like, depending on the amount of chilli powder you include.

SERVES 4–6

1 onion, chopped

1¹/₂ tbsp Garlic and Ginger Paste (see page 27)

400 g/14 oz large, juicy tomatoes, peeled and chopped,
  or canned tomatoes

¹/₄–¹/₂ tsp chilli powder

pinch of sugar

salt and pepper

30 g/1 oz Ghee (see page 253) or 2 tbsp vegetable
  or groundnut oil

125 ml/4 fl oz water

1 tbsp tomato purée

40 g/1¹/₂ oz butter, cut into small pieces

¹/₂ tsp Garam Masala (see page 251)

¹/₂ tsp ground cumin

¹/₂ tsp ground coriander

1 cooked Tandoori Chicken (see page 156), cut
  into 8 pieces

4 tbsp double cream

to garnish

4 tbsp cashew nuts, lightly toasted and chopped

fresh coriander sprigs, to garnish

1 Put the onion and garlic and ginger paste in a food processor, blender or spice grinder and whiz together until a paste forms. Add the tomatoes, chilli powder, the sugar and a pinch of salt and whiz again until blended.

2 Melt the ghee in a kadhai, wok or large frying pan over a medium-high heat. Add the tomato mixture and water, stirring in the tomato purée.

3 Bring the mixture to the boil, stirring, then reduce the heat to very low and simmer for 5 minutes, stirring occasionally, until the sauce thickens.

4 Stir in half the butter, the garam masala, cumin and coriander. Add the chicken pieces and stir around until they are well coated. Simmer for about 10 minutes longer, or until the chicken is hot. Taste and adjust the seasoning, if necessary.

5 Lightly beat the cream in a small bowl and stir in several tablespoons of the hot sauce, beating constantly. Stir the cream mixture into the tomato sauce, then add the remaining butter and stir until it melts. Garnish with the chopped cashew nuts and coriander and serve straight from the pan.

160

quick chicken curry with mushrooms and beans
murgh mushroom rasedaar

A quick-and-easy, rich curry that takes less time to prepare than more traditional Indian dishes.

SERVES 4–6

55 g/2 oz Ghee (see page 253) or 4 tbsp vegetable
   or groundnut oil

8 skinless, boneless chicken thighs, sliced

1 small onion, chopped

2 large garlic cloves, crushed

100 g/3½ oz green beans, topped and tailed and chopped

100 g/3½ oz mushrooms, thickly sliced

2 tbsp milk

salt and pepper

fresh coriander sprigs, to garnish

for the curry paste

2 tsp Garam Masala (see page 251)

1 tsp mild, medium or hot curry powder, to taste

1 tbsp water

1 To make the curry paste, put the garam masala and curry powder in a bowl and stir in the water, then set aside.

2 Melt half the ghee in a large, heavy-based saucepan or frying pan with a tight-fitting lid over a medium-high heat. Add the chicken pieces and curry paste and stir around for 5 minutes.

3 Add the onion, garlic and green beans and continue cooking for a further 5 minutes until the chicken is cooked through and the juices run clear.

4 Add the remaining ghee and mushrooms and, when the ghee melts, stir in the milk. Season to taste with salt and pepper. Reduce the heat to low, cover and simmer for 10 minutes, stirring occasionally.

chicken tikka masala

murgh tikka makhani

This Indian dish reputedly started life in London restaurants as a way to use up leftover cooked tandoori chicken. It has now gone full cycle and is prepared in Indian restaurants. The quickest way to make this is to buy cooked tandoori chicken pieces from a supermarket or an Indian take-away. If, however, you want to make your own tandoori chicken, follow the recipe on page 156, then cut the cooked bird into pieces.

SERVES 4–6

400 g/14 oz canned chopped tomatoes

300 ml/10 fl oz double cream

8 pieces cooked tandoori chicken (see page 156)

fresh coriander sprigs, to garnish

for the tikka masala

30 g/1 oz Ghee (see page 253) or 2 tbsp vegetable
  or groundnut oil

1 large garlic clove, finely chopped

1 fresh red chilli, deseeded and chopped

2 tsp ground cumin

2 tsp ground paprika

¹/₂ tsp salt

black pepper

1 To make the tikka masala, melt the ghee or heat the oil in a large frying pan with a lid over a medium heat. Add the garlic and chilli and stir-fry for 1 minute. Stir in the cumin, paprika, salt and pepper to taste and continue stirring for about 30 seconds.

2 Stir the tomatoes with their juices and the cream into the pan. Reduce the heat to low and leave the sauce to simmer for about 10 minutes, stirring frequently, until it reduces and thickens.

3 Meanwhile, remove all the bones and any skin from the tandoori chicken pieces, then cut the meat into bite-size pieces.

4 Adjust the seasoning of the sauce, if necessary. Add the chicken pieces to the pan, cover and leave to simmer for 3–5 minutes until the chicken is heated through. Sprinkle with the coriander to serve.

162

kashmiri chicken
murgh kashmiri

This mild and aromatic Kashmiri dish is delicately flavoured and coloured with saffron threads, grown in the northern region. Chicken thighs are used in this recipe, but any pieces of boneless meat are suitable.

SERVES 4–6

seeds from 8 green cardamom pods

$^1/_2$ tsp coriander seeds

$^1/_2$ tsp cumin seeds

1 cinnamon stick

8 black peppercorns

6 cloves

1 tbsp hot water

$^1/_2$ tsp saffron threads

40 g/1$^1/_2$ oz Ghee (see page 253) or 3 tbsp vegetable
  or groundnut oil

1 large onion, finely chopped

2 tbsp Garlic and Ginger Paste (see page 27)

250 ml/9 fl oz natural yogurt

8 skinless, boneless chicken thighs, sliced

3 tbsp ground almonds

55 g/2 oz blanched pistachio nuts, finely chopped

2 tbsp chopped fresh coriander

2 tbsp chopped fresh mint*

salt

toasted flaked almonds, to garnish

1 Dry-roast the cardamom seeds in a hot frying pan over a medium-low heat, stirring constantly, until you can smell the aroma. Immediately tip them out of the pan so they don't burn. Repeat with the coriander and cumin seeds, cinnamon, peppercorns and cloves. Put all the spices, except the cinnamon stick, in a spice grinder or pestle and mortar and grind to a powder.

2 Put the water and saffron threads in a small bowl and set aside.

3 Melt the ghee in a flameproof casserole or large frying pan with a tight-fitting lid. Add the onion and fry, stirring occasionally, over a medium-high heat for 5–8 minutes until it becomes golden brown. Add the garlic and ginger paste and continue stirring for 2 minutes.

4 Stir in the ground spices* and the cinnamon stick. Take the onion mixture off the heat and mix in the yogurt, a small amount at a time, stirring vigorously with each addition, then return to the heat and continue stirring for 2–3 minutes until the ghee separates. Add the chicken pieces.

5 Bring the mixture to the boil, stirring constantly, then reduce the heat to the lowest setting, cover the pan and simmer for 20 minutes, stirring occasionally and checking that the mixture isn't catching on the base of the pan. If it does start to catch, stir in a few tablespoons of water.

6 Stir the ground almonds, pistachios, saffron liquid, half the coriander, all the mint leaves and salt, to taste, into the chicken. Re-cover the pan and continue simmering for about 5 minutes until the chicken is tender and the sauce is thickened. Sprinkle with the remaining coriander and almonds.

*cook's tips

The mint leaves add a wonderful aroma to the dish in Step 6 but, unfortunately, the heat turns them an unappetizing dark colour. That is why extra fresh coriander is sprinkled over the dish just before serving.

This rich dish is very mild, making it ideal for anyone new to Indian food who is worried about the food being too spicy. However, $1/4$–$1/2$ teaspoon chilli powder can be added with the other ground spices in Step 4 for anyone who likes more heat.

chicken jalfrezi
murgh jalfrezi

Bangladeshi cooks are credited with bringing this popular restaurant dish to Britain. Walk along Brick Lane in the heart of London's Bangladeshi community and each of the numerous restaurants will claim to serve the most 'authentic' version.

SERVES 4–6

55 g/2 oz Ghee (see page 253) or 4 tbsp vegetable
  or groundnut oil

8 skinless, boneless chicken thighs, sliced

1 large onion, chopped

2 tbsp Garlic and Ginger Paste (see page 27)

2 green peppers, cored, deseeded and chopped

1 large fresh green chilli, deseeded and finely chopped

1 tsp ground cumin

1 tsp ground coriander

$^1/_4$–$^1/_2$ tsp chilli powder

$^1/_2$ tsp ground turmeric

$^1/_4$ tsp salt

400 g/14 oz canned chopped tomatoes

125 ml/4 fl oz water

chopped fresh coriander, to garnish

1 Melt half the ghee in a kadhai, wok or large frying pan over a medium-high heat. Add the chicken pieces and stir around for 5 minutes until browned, but not necessarily cooked through, then remove from the pan with a slotted spoon and set aside.

2 Melt the remaining ghee in the pan. Add the onion and fry, stirring frequently, for 5–8 minutes until golden brown. Stir in the garlic and ginger paste and continue frying for 2 minutes, stirring frequently.

3 Add the peppers to the pan and stir around for 2 minutes.

4 Stir in the chilli, cumin, coriander, chilli powder, turmeric and salt. Add the tomatoes with their juice and the water* and bring to the boil.

5 Reduce the heat to low, add the chicken and leave it to simmer, uncovered, for 10 minutes, stirring frequently, until the peppers are tender, the chicken is cooked through and the juices run clear if you pierce a few pieces with the tip of a knife. Sprinkle with the coriander.

*cook's tip
To make this into a more filling meal that doesn't need any accompanying rice, add 400 g/14 oz chopped new potatoes with the tomatoes and water in Step 4. Bring to the boil, then reduce the heat and simmer for 5 minutes before you add the chicken.

SEAFOOD DISHES

168 Mumbai's bustling Sassoon Docks is actually one of India's largest fish markets, and each morning it is possible to see some of the bounty yielded from more than 6000 kilometres of coastline, along with the catch from inland rivers, reservoirs, lakes and southern backwaters.

Fishermen bring their catch on land for sale on the spot, for transporting around India or for quick freezing before international shipping. It's a dazzling display that includes everything from huge tuna and sharks to tiny whitebait and prawns, mussels and clams. Not necessarily for the faint-hearted, shimmering colours and blood and guts set the scene for hundreds of thousands of rupees to change hands, as restaurateurs, wholesalers and home cooks look for the freshest and best bargains.

Bengal in the east and Goa and Kerala along the western Malabar coast are particularly known for their fresh seafood preparations, but, as in all aspects of Indian cooking, each region has its preferred style of flavouring and cooking. Fresh coconut flavours many dishes from Goa and Kerala, while mustard oil and mustard seeds are often used along with coconut in Bengal.

Bengalis, considered India's best seafood cooks, think nothing of eating fish and rice once or twice a day. Pomfret in Chilli Yogurt (see page 189) is an example of the popular dishes served in Kolkata, where the colourful Bag Bazaar Market provides the city's cooks with fresh seafood. Fish Pakoras (see page 190), fried in a light chickpea flour batter, are a tasty *chaat* fried at the snack bars around the market. Serve with Coriander Chutney (see page 245) to go with pre-dinner drinks. For a really quick-and-easy recipe that is equally good served hot or at room temperature, Pickled Mackerel (see page 186) with fried whole seeds is difficult to beat.

The photogenic ancient Chinese fishing nets of Fort Kochi are an icon in Kerala and have been bringing in the daily catch for more than 600 years, as well as a daily pull of tourists today. It's almost impossible to eat fresher seafood than at the numerous eating shacks situated alongside the fishing nets. The just-caught fish is displayed for selection, then cooked and flavoured to order. Mussels with Mustard Seeds and Shallots (see page 177), which is equally delicious made with the large local prawns, could be one of the quickly cooked dishes.

For Kerala's fishermen, who set out in the middle of the night, breakfast or lunch may well be a *molee*, the region's most popular fish stew flavoured with coconut. It will be cooked on board with whatever fish the day's catch has provided. Nothing is wasted and heads and tails go into the pot, along with coconut milk and spices. The final dish can be very hot or mild, all depending on the cook's preference. For a slightly more refined mixed seafood curry, try the Goan-style Seafood Curry (see page 182) with a mixture of prawns and white fish in a creamy, spiced coconut broth, coloured with vibrant turmeric.

Any visit to tranquil Goa has to include sampling the fresh fish dishes that are cooked all day and late into the night at the numerous open-air beach shacks. Prawns, mussels, pomfret, crabs and lobsters are among the variety cooked to order.

Fishermen's wives are often in charge of sorting and selling the day's catch

For a taste of the Malabar coast, try pomfret

Indian cooks, especially in the coastal communities, have many recipes for cooking individual portions of fish wrapped in banana leaves, and the aromatic steamed version on page 178 comes from Mumbai's Parsi community. Each piece of fish is smeared with fresh coriander chutney before it is wrapped to provide the most wonderful aromas when the parcels are opened at the table.

As Indian restaurants have proliferated outside the country, the availability of specific fish from Indian waters has followed. Many specimens are now sold frozen at supermarkets. For a taste of the Malabar Coast, try pomfret, a delicately flavoured white fish that is popular on the subcontinent. It tastes similar to sole, and can be grilled, fried or baked. Other particular Indian specialities to look for include pearlspot, also from the Malabar coast, and goat fish, with a shimmering rosy red skin that looks like red mullet.

As anyone who has ever ordered Bombay duck in an Indian or Chinese restaurant knows, it has never had webbed feet or a flat bill. It's actually a small, translucent fish that is salted and hung to dry in the hot Mumbai sun. It is then sold mostly as a snack, or to be crumbled and sprinkled over other dishes for extra flavour.

As with all fish recipes from anywhere in the world, Indian recipes rely on ultra-fresh seafood. Fish should never smell of anything other than a slight hint of the sea, the eyes should be clear and the gills bright red. Any frozen fish should be cooked on the day it is thawed.

Right *Fresh swordfish can be bought on the beach*

Overleaf *Fishermen haul in their fishing nets on one of Goa's sandy beaches*

tandoori prawns
tandoori jhinga

Quick and easy, this is one of the ways large tiger prawns are cooked in ramshackle-looking beach shacks along the Goan coast. Locals and tourists alike stroll along the sandy beaches and stop for just-cooked fish and shellfish served the way it always should be: ultra-fresh and simply cooked.

SERVES 4

4 tbsp natural yogurt

2 fresh green chillies, deseeded and chopped

1/2 tbsp Garlic and Ginger Paste (see page 27)

seeds from 4 green cardamom pods

2 tsp ground cumin

1 tsp tomato purée

1/4 tsp ground turmeric

1/4 tsp salt

pinch of chilli powder, ideally Kashmiri chilli powder

24 raw tiger prawns, thawed if frozen, peeled, deveined and tails left intact

lemon or lime wedges, to serve

1 Put the yogurt, chillies and garlic and ginger paste in a small food processor, spice grinder or pestle and mortar and whiz until a paste forms. Transfer the paste to a large non-metallic bowl and stir in the cardamom seeds, cumin, tomato purée, turmeric, salt and chilli powder*.

2 Add the prawns to the bowl and use your hands to make sure they are coated with the yogurt marinade. Cover the bowl with clingfilm and chill for at least 30 minutes, or up to 4 hours.

3 When you are ready to cook, heat a large, flat tava, griddle or frying pan over a high heat until a few drops of water 'dance' when they hit the surface. Use crumpled kitchen paper or a pastry brush to very lightly grease the hot pan with oil.

4 Use tongs to lift the prawns out of the marinade, letting the excess drip back into the bowl, then place the prawns on the tava and leave them to fry for 2 minutes. Flip the prawns over and fry for 1–2 minutes longer until they turn pink, curl and are opaque all the way through when you cut one. Serve at once with lemon or lime wedges for squeezing over.

*cook's tip

The spiced yogurt mixture also makes an excellent marinade for tandoori seafood kebabs. Cut 750 g/1 lb 10 oz thick, meaty fillets of white fish, such as cod, halibut or monkfish, into 4-cm/1½-inch cubes and put in the marinade with 12 or 16 large peeled and deveined prawns. Leave to marinate for at least 30 minutes or up to 4 hours. When ready to cook, preheat the grill to medium-high or light barbecue coals and leave until they turn grey. Thread the fish and prawns on to 6 long, flat greased metal skewers, alternating with pieces of blanched red or green peppers and/or button mushrooms. Grill for about 15 minutes, turning the skewers and brushing with any leftover marinade frequently, until the fish flakes and the edges of the fish are lightly charred.

mussels with mustard seeds and shallots 177
tissario kadugu

Baskets piled high with fresh mussels are not an uncommon slight along India's southern Malabar coast. Quickly cooked, fragrant dishes coloured with golden turmeric like this are served in the open-air restaurants along Kochi's harbourside, opposite the picturesque Chinese fishing nets.

SERVES 4

2 kg/4 lb 8 oz live mussels in their shells

3 tbsp vegetable or groundnut oil

¹/₂ tbsp black mustard seeds

8 shallots, chopped

2 garlic cloves, crushed

2 tbsp distilled vinegar

4 small fresh red chillies

85 g/3 oz creamed coconut, dissolved in
   300 ml/10 fl oz boiling water

10 fresh curry leaves or 1 tbsp dried

¹/₂ tsp ground turmeric

¹/₄–¹/₂ tsp chilli powder

salt

1 Pick over the mussels and discard any with broken shells or any open ones that do not close when firmly tapped. Scrub the mussels under cold running water to remove any barnacles and use a small knife to remove the 'beards', if necessary, then set aside.

2 Heat the oil in a kadhai, wok or large frying pan over a medium-high heat. Add the mustard seeds and stir them around for about 1 minute, or until they start to jump.

3 Add the shallots and garlic cloves and fry, stirring frequently, for 3 minutes, or until they start to brown. Stir in the vinegar, whole chillies, dissolved coconut, the curry leaves, turmeric, chilli powder and a pinch of salt and bring to the boil, stirring.

4 Reduce the heat to very low. Add the mussels, cover the pan and leave the mussels to simmer, shaking the pan frequently, for 3–4 minutes, or until they are all open. Discard any that remain closed. Ladle the mussels into deep bowls, then taste the broth* and add extra salt, if necessary. Spoon over the mussels and serve.

*cook's tip
Taste the bright yellow broth before you add it to the mussels in Step 4. If the mussels were gritty, sieve the liquid through a sieve lined with muslin or kitchen paper. Mussels should be cooked on the day of purchase. When raw mussels don't close or cooked ones don't open, it is an indication that they aren't fresh or are dead. They must not be eaten.

178 # steamed fish with coriander chutney
paatrani machchi

*Kerala's numerous tranquil backwaters are lined
with elegant coconut trees, and the large leaves are
often used in cooking or as a serving plate. Here, the
glossy green leaves are wrapped around fresh fish
fillets with a fresh-tasting chutney to keep the fish
moist while it cooks. When these parcels are opened
at the table, the vibrant flavours of southern India
are unmistakable.*

SERVES 4

1 quantity Coriander Chutney (see page 245)

1 large fresh banana leaf*

vegetable or groundnut oil

4 white fish fillets, such as pomfret or sole, about
   140 g/5 oz each

salt and pepper

lime or lemon wedges, to serve

1 Prepare the coriander chutney recipe at least 2
hours in advance to allow the flavours to blend.

2 Meanwhile, cut the banana leaf into 4 squares that
are large enough to fold comfortably around the
fish to make tight parcels, about 25 cm/10 inches square.

3 Working with one piece of leaf at a time, very
lightly rub the bottom with oil. Put one of the
fish fillets in the centre of the oiled side, flesh-side up.
Spread one quarter of the coriander chutney over the
top and season to taste with salt and pepper.

4 Fold one side of the leaf over the fish, then fold the
opposite side over. Turn the leaf so the folded edges
are top and bottom. Fold the right-hand end of the leaf
parcel into the centre, then fold over the left-hand side.
Trim the ends if the parcel becomes too bulky.

5 Use 2 wooden skewers to close the leaf parcel.
Repeat with the remaining ingredients and banana
leaf squares. The fish parcels can now be refrigerated for
several hours.

6 When you are ready to cook the fish, place a
steamer large enough to hold the parcels in a single
layer over a pan of boiling water, without letting the
water touch the fish. Add the fish, cover the pan and
steam for 15 minutes. Test by opening 1 parcel to make
sure the fish is cooked through and flakes easily.

7 Serve the wrapped parcels with lime or lemon
wedges and allow each guest to open their own to
release the wonderful aromas.

*cook's tip

Fresh banana leaves are sold in the chilled cabinet
of many Asian food shops. One large one should be
sufficient for the 4 squares needed for this recipe, but
it might be necessary to buy 2. If you can't find banana
leaves, use kitchen foil, shiny-side up. Just take care
to seal the edges tightly so none of the fragrant juices
seep out.

The banana-leaf squares will be easier to fold if they
are briefly dipped in a bowl of very hot water until they
feel pliable. The banana leaves should be completely
dried, however, before you add the oil in Step 3.

balti fish curry
machchli masala

This is for those who prefer robustly flavoured dishes, more like the ones served in northern India, than the coconut-based ones from the south.

SERVES 4–6

900 g/2 lb thick fish fillets, such as monkfish, grey mullet, cod or haddock, rinsed and cut into large chunks

2 bay leaves, torn

140 g/5 oz Ghee (see page 253) or 150 ml/5 fl oz vegetable or groundnut oil

2 large onions, chopped

1/2 tbsp salt

150 ml/5 fl oz water

chopped fresh coriander, to garnish

for the marinade

1/2 tbsp Garlic and Ginger Paste (see page 27)

1 fresh green chilli, deseeded and chopped

1 tsp ground coriander

1 tsp ground cumin

1/2 tsp ground turmeric

1/4–1/2 tsp chilli powder

salt

1 tbsp water

1 To make the marinade, mix the garlic and ginger paste, green chilli, ground coriander, cumin, turmeric and chilli powder together with salt, to taste, in a large bowl. Gradually stir in the water to form a thin paste. Add the fish chunks and smear with the marinade. Tuck the bay leaves underneath and leave to marinate in the refrigerator for at least 30 minutes, or up to 4 hours.

2 When you are ready to cook the fish, remove from the refrigerator 15 minutes in advance. Melt the ghee in a kadhai, wok or large frying pan over a medium-high heat. Add the onion, sprinkle with the salt and fry, stirring frequently, for 8 minutes, or until it is very soft and golden*.

3 Gently add the fish and bay leaves to the pan and stir in the water. Bring to the boil, then immediately reduce the heat and cook the fish for 4–5 minutes, spooning the sauce over the fish and carefully moving the chunks around, until they are cooked through and the flesh flakes easily. Adjust the seasoning, if necessary, and sprinkle with coriander.

*cook's tip
Do not over-brown the onions in Step 2 or the dish will taste bitter. They should be golden, but not brown, when the fish is added.

goan-style seafood curry
goa che nalla chi kadi

With mustard seeds, curry leaves and a creamy coconut sauce, this quick-and-easy dish could easily have originated anywhere in southern India, not just in tropical Goa on the west coast. But it is in Goa that the coconut is king: the flesh and milk are used in sweet and savoury dishes, and the carved shells are popular tourist souvenirs.

SERVES 4–6

3 tbsp vegetable or groundnut oil

1 tbsp black mustard seeds

12 fresh curry leaves or 1 tbsp dried

6 shallots, finely chopped*

1 garlic clove, crushed

1 tsp ground turmeric

$^1/_2$ ground coriander

$^1/_4$–$^1/_2$ tsp chilli powder

140 g/5 oz creamed coconut, grated and dissolved in 300 ml/10 fl oz boiling water

500 g/1 lb 2 oz skinless, boneless white fish, such as monkfish or cod, cut into large chunks

450 g/1 lb large raw prawns, peeled and deveined

finely grated rind and juice of 1 lime

salt

lime wedges, to serve

1 Heat the oil in a kadhai, wok or large frying pan over a high heat. Add the mustard seeds and stir them around for about 1 minute, or until they jump. Stir in the curry leaves.

2 Add the shallots and garlic and stir for about 5 minutes, or until the shallots are golden. Stir in the turmeric, coriander and chilli powder and continue stirring for about 30 seconds.

3 Add the dissolved creamed coconut. Bring to the boil, then reduce the heat to medium and stir for about 2 minutes.

4 Reduce the heat to low, add the fish and simmer for 1 minute, stirring the sauce over the fish and very gently stirring it around. Add the prawns and continue to simmer for 4–5 minutes longer until the fish flesh flakes easily and the prawns turn pink and curl.

5 Add half the lime juice, then taste and add more lime juice and salt to taste. Sprinkle with the lime rind and serve with lime wedges.

*cook's tip

Peeling a large number of shallots like this can be fiddly, but the job is quicker if you submerge them in a pan of boiling water for 30–45 seconds. Drain the shallots and use a knife to slice off the root end, then they should peel easily.

prawn pooris
jhinga puri

This restaurant favourite is easy to re-create at home. The deep-fried Pooris aren't difficult to make, but remember to leave enough time for the dough to rest for 20 minutes before it is fried. Serve this as a starter or main course or make mini Pooris and serve the prawn mixture as a dip.

SERVES 6

2 tsp coriander seeds

$^1/_2$ tsp black peppercorns

1 large garlic clove, crushed

1 tsp ground turmeric

$^1/_4$–$^1/_2$ tsp chilli powder

$^1/_2$ tsp salt

40 g/1$^1/_2$ oz Ghee (see page 253) or 3 tbsp vegetable
   or groundnut oil

1 onion, grated

800 g/1 lb 12 oz canned crushed tomatoes

pinch of sugar

500 g/1 lb 2 oz small, cooked peeled prawns,
   thawed if frozen

$^1/_2$ tsp Garam Masala (see page 251), plus extra
   to garnish

$^1/_2$ quantity Pooris* (see page 240), kept warm

fresh coriander, to garnish

1 Put the coriander seeds, peppercorns, garlic, turmeric, chilli powder and salt in a small food processor, spice grinder or pestle and mortar and blend to a thick paste.

2 Melt the ghee in a kadhai, wok or large frying pan over a medium-low heat. Add the paste and fry, stirring constantly, for about 30 seconds.

3 Add the grated onion and stir around for a further 30 seconds. Stir in the tomatoes and their juice and the sugar. Bring to the boil, stirring, and leave to bubble for 10 minutes, mashing the tomatoes against the side of the pan to break them down, or until reduced. Taste and add extra salt, if necessary.

4 Add the prawns and sprinkle with the garam masala. When the prawns are hot, arrange the hot pooris on plates and top each one with a portion of the prawns. Sprinkle with the coriander and garam masala.

*cook's tip

Deep-fried pooris are best served straight from the pan, so it is a good idea to have a couple of pans to use if you are entertaining. The pooris, with their rich, light texture, are traditional with this dish, but chapatis or naans are also good, especially if you want to avoid last-minute deep-frying.

pickled mackerel
bhangde lonchen

This quick and crunchy dish is equally good served hot, straight from the pan, or when cooled to room temperature.

SERVES 4

vegetable or groundnut oil

finely grated rind and juice of 1 lime

salt and pepper

4 large mackerel fillets, about 175 g/6 oz each*

1¹/₂ tsp cumin seeds

1¹/₂ tsp black mustard seeds

1¹/₂ tsp nigella seeds

1¹/₂ tsp fennel seeds

1¹/₂ tsp coriander seeds

4-cm/1¹/₂-inch piece of fresh root ginger, very
   finely chopped

1¹/₂ garlic cloves, very finely chopped

3 shallots, very finely chopped

pinch of chilli powder

very finely sliced deseeded fresh red chillies, to garnish

lime wedges, to serve

1 Mix together 2 tablespoons of oil, the lime rind and juice and salt and pepper, to taste, in a non-metallic bowl that will hold the mackerel fillets in a flat layer. Add the mackerel fillets and use your hands to cover them in the marinade, then set aside for at least 10 minutes, or cover and chill for up to 4 hours.

2 Meanwhile, preheat the grill to high, and lightly brush the grill with oil.

3 Remove the mackerel from the refrigerator 15 minutes in advance. Put the mackerel on the grill, skin-side down, and grill about 10 cm/4 inches from the source of the heat for 6 minutes, or until the flesh is cooked through when pierced with the tip of a knife and flakes easily.

4 While the mackerel grills, heat 2 tablespoons of the oil in a kadhai, wok or large frying pan over a medium-high heat. Add the cumin, black mustard seeds, nigella, fennel and coriander seeds and stir around until the black mustard seeds start to jump and the coriander and cumin seeds just start to brown. Immediately remove the pan from the heat and stir in the ginger, garlic, shallots and chilli powder and continue stirring for 1 minute.

5 Transfer the mackerel fillets to plates and spoon the spice mixture over. Garnish with red chilli slices and serve with lime wedges for squeezing over.

*cook's tip
The spicy flavour of this recipe works well with any oily fish fillets, so try herring, salmon and tuna as well.

Seafood is an important part of the everyday Bengali diet, where this dish using pomfret fillets originates. Pomfret, with its excellent flavour and delicate texture, is one of the jewels of Indian seafood cooking. It is now available at large supermarket fish counters, but plaice or sole can be substituted.

pomfret in chilli yogurt
dahi pamplet

5 Melt the ghee in the wiped pan over a medium-high heat. When it is bubbling, turn the heat to medium and add the fillets in a single layer. Fry for 2½ minutes, or until golden, then turn them over.

6 Continue frying for a further minute, then return the yogurt sauce to the pan and reheat, stirring. When the fillets flake easily and are cooked through and the sauce is hot, transfer to plates and sprinkle with the chilli.

SERVES 4

2 tbsp vegetable or groundnut oil

1 large onion, sliced

4-cm/1½-inch piece of fresh root ginger, finely chopped

½ tsp salt

¼ tsp ground turmeric

pinch of ground cinnamon

pinch of ground cloves

200 ml/7 fl oz natural yogurt

1 tbsp plain flour

small pinch of chilli powder

salt and pepper

4 skinless pomfret fillets, about 150 g/5½ oz each, wiped dry

30 g/1 oz Ghee (see page 253) or 2 tbsp vegetable or groundnut oil

2 fresh fat green chillies, deseeded and finely chopped

1 Heat the oil in a large frying pan over a medium-high heat. Add the onion and fry, stirring, for 8 minutes, or until it is soft and dark golden brown. Add the ginger and stir around for a further 1 minute.

2 Stir in the salt, turmeric, cinnamon and cloves and continue stirring for 30 seconds. Remove the pan from the heat and stir in the yogurt, a little at a time, beating constantly.

3 Transfer the yogurt mixture to a blender or food processor and whiz until a paste forms.

4 Season the flour with chilli powder and salt and pepper to taste. Place it on a plate and lightly dust the fish fillets on both sides.

Indian seafood is fished from rivers and backwaters, as well as the west and east coasts

190
fish pakoras
machchli pakora

After a morning's stroll through the ancient town of Kochi in Kerala, simple, fried-to-order pakoras like these make a relaxing lunch by the harbourside fish market. These are ideal for a quick family meal or as a snack to enjoy with drinks.

SERVES 4–6

$^1/_2$ tsp salt

2 tbsp lemon juice or distilled white vinegar

pepper

700 g/1 lb 9 oz skinless white fish fillets, such as cod, halibut or monkfish, rinsed, patted dry and cut into large chunks

vegetable or groundnut oil, for deep-frying

lemon wedges, to serve

for the batter

140 g/5 oz besan or gram flour

seeds from 4 green cardamom pods

large pinch of ground turmeric

large pinch of bicarbonate of soda

finely grated rind of 1 lemon

salt and pepper

175 ml/6 fl oz water

1 Combine the salt, lemon juice and pepper, to taste, and rub all over the fish chunks, then set aside in a non-metallic bowl and leave to stand for 20–30 minutes.

2 Meanwhile, to make the batter* put the besan flour in a bowl and stir in the seeds from the cardamom pods, turmeric, bicarbonate of soda, lemon rind and salt and pepper to taste. Make a well in the centre and gradually stir in the water until a thin batter similar to single cream forms.

3 Gently stir the pieces of fish into the batter, taking care not to break them up.

4 Heat enough oil for deep-frying in a kadhai, wok, deep-fat fryer or large heavy-based saucepan to 180°C/350°F, or until a cube of bread browns in 30 seconds. Remove the fish pieces from the batter and let the excess batter drip back into the bowl. Without overcrowding the pan, drop fish pieces in the hot fat and fry for about 2$^1/_2$–3 minutes until golden brown.

5 Immediately use a slotted spoon to remove the fried fish pieces from the fat and drain on crumpled kitchen paper. Continue until all the fish is fried, then serve hot with the lemon wedges.

* cook's tip
The batter can be made several hours in advance and set aside covered with clingfilm. Stir it well before using, and add a little extra water if it has become too thick. If the batter is too thick it will remain raw next to the fish.

DESSERTS
& DRINKS

194 It is somewhat ironic that Indians are known around the world for their love of sweet food, yet don't eat desserts on a daily basis. Instead, family meals are more likely to end with a plate of prepared fresh fruit, selected for its seasonal availability. What Indians do find irresistible, however, is the colourful and appealing display of sweetmeats sold in the numerous *mithai*, sweet shops, especially in the crowded cities.

Bengalis are known for their sweetmeat preparations, and congregating at *mithai* shops is a part of daily life in Kolkata. Decorating the sweetmeats with ultra-thin flecks of silver called *varak* only adds to the dazzling window displays.

When it comes to weddings, birthdays, religious celebrations and other special occasions, sweet desserts will be plentiful. The best-known Indian desserts are rich with dairy products or fried in ghee and a small amount often suffices.

At first glance, some of the most popular Indian desserts appear similar to their western counterparts, but when you read the recipes it becomes clear these are uniquely Indian. From northern India, Kheer (see page 200), the traditional rice pudding, is flavoured with cardamom, topped with nuts and occasionally silver *varak*, a reflection of the days it was served at Moghul banquets. Indian Kheer, slowly simmered on the hob, is much sweeter and richer than rice puddings in Europe or America. This dessert is often part of Hindu feasts, as the god Rama is said to have been conceived after his mother ate a divine portion of Kheer.

Whereas European bread puddings are everyday desserts for family meals, *shahi tukda*, the Indian Bread Pudding (see page 206), is fried in ghee and flavoured and coloured with cardamom and saffron, a legacy from the days it was served in Moghul courts. It is too rich to eat except on special occasions.

European cooking has used the sweetness of carrots and parsnips to flavour desserts since medieval times, but nothing comes close to the rich and filling Carrot Halva (see page 203) from the Punjab and Gujarat. Flavoured with cardamom and pistachios, this is a must at Hindu and Sikh weddings, when it is usually finished with a final *varak* decoration. It can be served hot or cold, with or without cream or ice cream. When made in Gujarat, the bright red-orange carrots that grow there give this dessert a deep, jewel-like colour.

For a creamy, rich elegance, few desserts surpass the strained yogurt mixture of Shrikhand with Pomegranate (see page 207), the name of which translates as 'ambrosia of the gods'. The subtle flavouring of cardamom and saffron transform this surprisingly economical dessert into something very special. In Maharashtra, Shrikhand is traditionally accompanied by just-fried Pooris (see page 240), but it is also fantastic served with fresh tropical fruit, such as mango, passion fruit, melon or even more everyday plantains or bananas.

Another economical Indian dessert that tastes rich and extravagant is Payasam (see page 201) from the south. Vermicelli noodles, like Italian angel hair pasta, are simmered in sweetened milk with nuts. During the month-long Muslim festival of Ramadan, this is often included in the feast that breaks the day's fast.

Kulfi, the Indian ice cream that is traditionally frozen in tall, cone-shaped moulds, is a firm favourite with young and old alike everywhere in India. It's difficult to find anyone who doesn't devour this extra-sweet chilled dessert, but it isn't quite as easy to find anyone who actually makes it at home. Although not difficult, there isn't much point in India as shops and roadside stalls sell it in almost every flavour imaginable. Try the version flavoured with almonds and saffron on page 204.

Alcoholic drinks are not a common part of Indian meals, except perhaps ice-cold Indian beer. Some states prohibit the sale of any alcohol, and when it is allowed, foreign wines and spirits are so heavily taxed that they become quite a luxury, even for tourists in

Left *A sweetmaker at work on his stall in Mysore in the province of Karnataka*

Overleaf *Women in festive dress attend one of the many religious festivals celebrated both nationally and locally*

It's difficult to find anyone who doesn't devour this extra-sweet chilled dessert

five-star hotels. Sparkling wine from Maharashtra, when available, goes surprising well with many spicy dishes. A more traditional option, however, is a glass of Salt Lassi (see page 212), the cooling yogurt and water drink that is like a raita in a glass. Mango Lassi (see page 213) is a refreshing version for a hot, sunny day, as is the sharp-tasting Ginger Cordial (see page 217), with a hint of lemon. Indians are great tea drinkers and Masala Tea (see page 214), flavoured with whole spices, is an everyday favourite. Drink it with milk or black. In India it is always served hot, but chilled it is a real thirst-quencher. The Pistachio and Almond Shake (see page 216) is like a liquid form of Kulfi. It's rich and thick and best served in small glasses.

200
kheer
kheer

One of the most popular desserts in India, kheer appears on all restaurant menus and is rarely missing from wedding feasts or Hindu and Muslim religious festivals. This rich, creamy dessert from northern India can be served hot or chilled, thick or very liquid with the rice floating in the milk, or flavoured with many different spices and fruit. Try this lightly spiced version chilled with fresh pineapple or mango slices for a treat.

SERVES 4–6
85 g/3 oz basmati rice
1.2 litres/2 pints milk
seeds from 4 green cardamom pods
1 cinnamon stick
100 g/3¹/₂ oz caster sugar, or to taste

to serve
grated jaggery or light brown sugar (optional)
chopped toasted pistachio nuts (optional)

1 Rinse the basmati rice in several changes of water until the water runs clear, then leave to soak for 30 minutes. Drain and set aside until ready to cook.

2 Rinse the saucepan with cold water and do not dry. Pour the milk into the pan, add the cardamom seeds and cinnamon stick and stir in the rice and sugar.

3 Put the pan over a medium-high heat and slowly bring to the boil, stirring. Reduce the heat to its lowest setting and leave the mixture to simmer, stirring frequently, for about 1 hour, until the rice is tender and the milky mixture has thickened. When the rice is tender you can stir in extra milk if you like the pudding with a soupier texture, or continue simmering if you like it thicker.

4 Spoon into individual bowls and sprinkle with jaggery to serve hot, or transfer to a bowl and leave to cool completely, stirring frequently. Cover and chill until ready to serve. Spoon the pudding into individual bowls and sprinkle with the nuts*.

*cook's tip
Transform this into a celebration dessert by decorating it with silver leaf.

payasam
payasam

This classic Indian pudding is made from very fine wheat noodles called sevian.

SERVES 4–6

30 g/1 oz Ghee (see page 253) or 2 tbsp vegetable or
   groundnut oil

175 g/6 oz sevian or vermicelli noodles, broken
   into 7.5-cm/3-inch pieces

40 g/1½ oz almonds or cashew nuts

1 litre/1¾ pints of milk

55 g/2 oz creamed coconut, crumbled

6 tbsp caster sugar

2 tbsp raisins or sultanas

pinch of salt

1 Melt the ghee in a kadhai, wok or large saucepan* over a medium heat. Add the sevian and stir for just 1–2 minutes until they turn a light golden brown. Use a slotted spoon to remove them from the pan and set aside.

2 Add the nuts to the pan and stir them around until they start to turn golden brown. Immediately stir in the milk, creamed coconut, sugar, raisins and salt.

3 Return the noodles to the pan. Bring the milk to the boil, then reduce the heat and simmer, uncovered and stirring almost constantly, for about 30 minutes, or until the noodles are tender and the milk is reduced. Taste and add extra sugar, if desired.

*cook's tip

If you don't have a kadhai or wok, use the widest saucepan you have. The wider the pan, the quicker the milk will reduce. Be sure to use a heavy-based pan, otherwise the milk might catch on the base and burn.

This is an example of the very sweet desserts most Indians adore. Originally from the Punjab and northern Indian, this rich, filling dessert can be served hot or chilled. In winter, it is often served hot with ice cream.

carrot halva
gajar ka halwa

SERVES 4–6

700 ml/1¼ pints milk

150 ml/5 fl oz single cream

500 g/1 lb 2 oz carrots, coarsely grated

85 g/3 oz caster sugar

1 tbsp dark brown sugar

55 g/2 oz Ghee (see page 253) or butter, melted

100 g/3½ oz ground almonds

seeds of 6 green cardamom pods, lightly crushed

3 tbsp raisins or sultanas

to decorate

chopped toasted blanched almonds and pistachios

silver leaf (optional)*

1 Rinse a large, heavy-based saucepan with cold water and do not dry. Pour the milk and cream into the pan, then stir in the carrots and put the pan over a high heat. Slowly bring to the boil, stirring.

2 Reduce the heat to its lowest setting and simmer, stirring frequently, for 2 hours, or until most of the milk has evaporated and the carrots are thickened.

3 Stir in the caster and dark brown sugars, then continue simmering for a further 30 minutes, stirring almost constantly to prevent the mixture from catching on the base of the pan.

4 Stir in the ghee, ground almonds, cardamom seeds and raisins. Continue simmering, stirring constantly, until the mixture is thick and there is a thin layer of ghee on the surface.

5 Stir the pudding well, then transfer to a serving dish. Sprinkle the surface with the nuts and add thin flecks of silver leaf, if you like.

*cook's tip

For an Indian wedding or other special occasion, the top of this dish will be decorated with the thinnest pieces of edible, pounded silver, called silver leaf or *varak*. It is sold in upmarket Indian food shops and is very easy to use. Each sheet of silver leaf has a paper backing. Put the silver side down on to the pudding, with the paper backing facing up, and use a paintbrush or pastry brush to dab on the paper. The silver will then transfer to the pudding. The trick is not to touch the silver with your fingers or it will stick.

Fruits and vegetables are very important parts of the Indian diet

204 saffron and almond kulfi
kesar badaam kulfi

Kulfi, or Indian ice cream, comes in a seemingly unlimited variety of flavours – just about all fresh fruit, nuts and spices are used. This version, flavoured with golden saffron, reflects the creamy dessert's Moghul heritage and ancient manuscripts describe a similar dessert being prepared for Emperor Akbar's lavish feasts in the late sixteenth and early seventeenth centuries. When you are served kulfi in India, it will have been frozen in a tall conical metal or plastic mould. These moulds are sold at Indian cookware shops, but you can use freezerproof ramekins instead.

MAKES 4

$^1/_2$ tsp saffron threads

75 ml/2$^1/_2$ fl oz milk

1 tbsp ground rice

$^1/_2$ tbsp ground almonds

225 ml/8 fl oz canned evaporated milk

225 ml/8 fl oz double cream

2 tbsp caster sugar

2 tbsp chopped toasted blanched almonds, to serve

1 Put the saffron threads in a dry frying pan over a high heat and 'toast', stirring frequently until you can smell the aroma, then immediately tip them out of the pan.

2 Put the milk in the frying pan over a medium-high heat, add the saffron threads and heat just until small bubbles appear around the edge. Remove the pan from the heat and leave the saffron to infuse for at least 15 minutes. Meanwhile, combine the ground rice and ground almonds in a heatproof bowl. Put a flat freezerproof container into the freezer.

3 Reheat the milk and saffron just until small bubbles appear around the edge, then slowly beat the milk into the almond mixture, beating until it is smooth without any lumps.

4 Pour the evaporated milk into a pan over a medium-high heat and bring to the boil, stirring. Remove the pan from the heat and stir into the milk mixture. Stir in the cream and sugar.

5 Return the pan to a medium heat and simmer, stirring constantly, for 5–10 minutes until it thickens, but do not boil. Remove the pan from the heat and set aside, stirring frequently, to cool.

6 Pour the saffron mixture into the freezerproof bowl and freeze for 30 minutes, then beat to break up any ice crystals. Continue beating every 30 minutes until the ice cream is thick and almost firm. If you are using metal kulfi moulds, put them in the freezer now.

7 Equally divide the mixture between 4 kulfi moulds or ramekins. Cover with the lid or clingfilm and freeze for at least 2 hours until solid.

8 To serve, dip a cloth in hot water, wring it out and rub it around the sides of the moulds or ramekins, then invert on to plates. Sprinkle with the toasted almonds and serve.

206
indian bread pudding
shahi tukda

From the tradition of lavish Moghul cooking in Hyderabad, this luscious bread pudding is flavoured and coloured with saffron.

SERVES 4–6

pinch of saffron threads

150 ml/5 fl oz double cream, plus extra to serve

150 ml/5 fl oz milk

55 g/2 oz caster sugar

seeds from 3 green cardamom pods

$^1/_2$ cinnamon stick

40 g/1$^1/_2$ oz dried mixed fruit, such as apricots, mangoes and figs, finely chopped

85 g/3 oz Ghee (see page 253) or 6 tbsp vegetable or groundnut oil

6 slices white bread, crusts removed and cut into triangles

freshly grated nutmeg, to garnish

1 Put the saffron threads in a dry saucepan over a high heat and 'toast', stirring frequently, until you can smell the aroma. Immediately tip them out of the pan.

2 Put the cream, milk, sugar, cardamom seeds, cinnamon and fruit in the saucepan over a medium-high heat. Add the saffron threads and heat just until small bubbles appear around the edge, stirring to dissolve the sugar. Remove the pan from the heat and leave the saffron to infuse for at least 15 minutes.

3 Meanwhile, preheat the oven to 200°C/400°F/Gas Mark 6 and lightly grease a 25 x 18-cm/10 x 7-inch ovenproof serving dish.

4 Melt a third of the ghee in a large frying pan over a medium-high heat. Add as many bread triangles as will fit in a single layer and fry until golden brown, then turn over and repeat on the other side. Remove from the pan and drain on some crumpled kitchen paper. Continue frying all the bread triangles, adding more ghee, as necessary.

5 Arrange the bread slices in the ovenproof dish and pour the cream and flavourings over, removing the cinnamon stick. Bake for 20 minutes, or until the top is golden brown. Leave to stand for a few minutes, then lightly grate fresh nutmeg over the top. Serve hot with chilled cream for pouring over.

The University and Rajbai Clock Tower overlook the Oval Maidan Park in Mumbai

This is the western Indian way of transforming everyday natural yogurt into a luscious, creamy dessert. Any fruit can be used for the topping, but it is a chance to enjoy the most exotic you can find. This is traditionally served with hot Pooris (see page 240), straight from the pan, although it is satisfying served on its own.

shrikhand with pomegranate
shrikhand anaari

207

SERVES 4

1 litre/1³/₄ pints natural yogurt

¹/₄ tsp saffron threads

2 tbsp milk

55 g/2 oz caster sugar, to taste

seeds of 2 green cardamom pods

2 pomegranates, or other exotic fruit

1 Line a sieve set over a bowl with a piece of muslin large enough to hang over the edge. Add the yogurt, then tie the corners of the muslin into a tight knot and tie them to a tap. Leave the bundle to hang over the sink for 4 hours, or until all the excess moisture drips away.

2 Put the saffron threads in a dry saucepan over a high heat and 'toast', stirring frequently, until you can smell the aroma. Immediately tip them out of the pan. Put the milk in the pan, return the saffron threads and warm just until bubbles appear around the edge, then set aside and leave to infuse.

3 When the yogurt is thick and creamy, put it in a bowl and stir in the sugar, cardamom pods and saffron-flavoured milk and beat until smooth. Taste and add extra sugar, if desired. Cover and chill for at least 1 hour until well chilled.

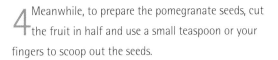

4 Meanwhile, to prepare the pomegranate seeds, cut the fruit in half and use a small teaspoon or your fingers to scoop out the seeds.

5 To serve, spoon the yogurt into individual bowls or plates and add the pomegranate seeds*.

*cook's tip
For a more everyday, family dessert, omit the saffron and cardamom seeds. Flavour the thickened yogurt with sugar and ground ginger and cinnamon, to taste, or top with sliced bananas or oranges. The yogurt is also good flavoured with vanilla seeds and extra sugar.

Overleaf *A woman sits overlooking the Ganges at Varanasi (Benares) in Uttar Pradesh Province*

210

spiced fruit salad
phal ki chaat

Fresh fruit, simply prepared, is often a welcome, light alternative to the traditional sweet Indian desserts. This refreshing, mildly spiced salad can be made with any fruit, and the more variety you include, the better. It makes a particularly good ending to a spicy meal.

SERVES 4–6

finely grated rind and juice of 1 lime

450 g/1 lb fresh fruit, such as bananas, guavas, oranges, kumquats, mangoes, melons and pineapple*

yogurt, to serve

for the spiced syrup

250 g/9 oz caster sugar

150 ml/5 fl oz water

1 vanilla pod, sliced lengthways, but left whole

1 cinnamon stick, broken in half

$^1/_2$ tsp fennel seeds

$^1/_2$ tsp black peppercorns, lightly crushed

$^1/_2$ tsp cumin seeds

1 Begin by making the spiced syrup. Put the sugar, half the water, vanilla pod, cinnamon stick, fennel seeds, peppercorns and cumin seeds into a small, heavy-based saucepan over a medium-high heat. Slowly bring to the boil, stirring to dissolve the sugar. As soon as the sugar boils, stop stirring and leave the syrup to bubble until it turns a golden brown.

2 Stand back from the pan and stir in the remaining water: the syrup will splash and splatter. Stir again to dissolve any caramel, then remove the pan from the heat and leave the syrup to cool slightly.

3 Meanwhile, put the lime rind and juice in a large, heatproof bowl. Prepare and cut each fruit as required and add it to the bowl. If you are using bananas, toss them immediately in the lime juice to prevent discoloration.

4 Pour in the syrup and leave the fruit and syrup to cool completely, then cover the bowl and chill for at least 1 hour before serving with thick, creamy yogurt.

*cook's tip

If you are including oranges, pineapples or any other juicy fruit, be sure to include the juice and squeeze the membranes and peels to extract extra juice. Work over the bowl when segmenting fruit to catch the juices.

salt lassi
namkeen lassi

'Salt lassi or sweet lassi?' This is the question anyone in India has to answer over and over. This chilled yogurt drink is universally popular and served everywhere, from the grandest hotels to the most humble beachside eating shacks. Many Indians drink lassi with meals, rather than beer or wine.

MAKES 4–6

700 ml/1¼ pints natural yogurt

½ tsp salt

¼ tsp sugar

250 ml/9 fl oz cold water

ice cubes

to garnish

ground cumin

fresh mint sprigs

1 Beat the yogurt, salt and sugar together in a jug or bowl, then add the water and whisk until frothy.

2 Fill 4 or 6 glasses with ice cubes and pour the yogurt mixture over. Lightly dust the top of each glass with ground cumin and garnish with mint*.

*cook's tip

For a sweet lassi, add 4 tablespoons sugar and omit the salt. You can also add ½–1 teaspoon rosewater, if you like. Pour over ice cubes and sprinkle with ground cumin and very finely chopped toasted pistachio nuts.

Water buffalo, used on farms all over India, here take a cooling dip

mango lassi 213
aam ki lassi

Cool and creamy, an ice-chilled mango lassi is unbeatable when temperatures are rising. For sweetness, many Indians say it is worth the effort of searching out an Alphonso mango, and to save time, you will find Alphonso mango pulp in cans in Indian food shops.

MAKES 4–6

1 large mango, ideally an Alphonso mango,
  coarsely chopped*
700 ml/1¼ pints natural yogurt
250 ml/9 fl oz cold water
2 tbsp caster sugar, or to taste
fresh lime juice, to taste
ice cubes
ground ginger, to decorate (optional)

1 Put 250 g/9 oz of the mango flesh in a food processor or blender with the yogurt and whiz until smooth (use any remaining mango for a fruit salad). Add the water and whiz again to blend.

2 The amount of sugar you will add depends on how sweet the mango is. Taste and stir in sugar to taste, then stir in the lime juice.

3 Fill 4 or 6 glasses with ice cubes and pour the mango mixture over. Lightly dust the top of each glass with ground ginger, if you like.

***cook's tip**

When buying fresh mangoes, look for an unblemished skin. A ripe mango will yield slightly when you squeeze it, and you can try to bring on an underripe fruit by placing it with an apple in a polythene bag with a few holes poked through. The larger the mango, the greater the fruit to seed ratio will be. Take care when you cut the mango, because mango juice can stain.

214 # masala tea
masalewali chai

There is always time for a cup of tea, or chai, *in India. Every office has a* chai walla, *and vendors sell it freshly brewed on street corners and train platforms. This milky version is drunk from the north to the south.*

MAKES 4–6 CUPS

1 litre/1³/₄ pints water

2.5-cm/1-inch piece of fresh root ginger, coarsely chopped

1 cinnamon stick

3 green cardamom pods, crushed

3 cloves

1¹/₂ tbsp Assam tea leaves

sugar, to taste

milk

1 Pour the water into a heavy-based saucepan over a medium-high heat. Add the ginger, cinnamon, cardamom and cloves and bring to the boil. Reduce the heat and simmer for 10 minutes.

2 Put the tea leaves in a teapot and pour over the water and spices. Stir and leave to infuse for 5 minutes*.

3 Strain the tea into teacups and add sugar and milk to taste.

*cook's tip

For iced masala tea, leave the tea to cool completely in Step 2, then strain into a jug and chill. Serve in tall glasses over ice cubes with sugar to taste and lemon or lime wedges for squeezing in.

Tea grows in India on the hills of Darjeeling, Assam and the Nilgiris and the leaves are picked by hand

216

pistachio and almond shake
pista-badaam doodh

The abundance of pistachios and almonds in India mean the combination is often included in both savoury and sweet dishes. Here the nuts are made into a thick, rich milk shake, which is served for celebrations such as birthdays. This takes time to cool, however, so make it in advance and keep it in the refrigerator until time to serve. Just be sure to stir well before pouring into glasses. This drink is so rich you will probably want to serve it in smaller glasses than for more familiar western milk shakes.

MAKES 4–6 SMALL GLASSES
pinch of saffron threads
70 g/2¹/₂ oz ground almonds
125 g/4¹/₂ oz pistachio nuts, very finely chopped
3 tbsp hot water
400 ml/14 fl oz condensed milk
pinch of salt
2–3 scoops ice cream

1 Put the saffron threads in a dry frying pan over a high heat and 'toast', stirring, until you can smell the aroma. Immediately tip them out of the pan.

2 Put the ground almonds, pistachio nuts and saffron threads in a spice grinder or large pestle and mortar and grind until a fine powder forms. Add the water and continue grinding until a paste forms.

3 Transfer the paste to a blender or food processor and add the condensed milk and salt. Whiz until blended, then add the ice cream to make a milk shake*. Transfer to a jug and chill until very cold. Stir well and serve.

*cook's tip
This mixture is so rich it can be frozen and served like an ice cream. After all the ingredients are incorporated in Step 3, transfer the mixture to a freezerproof container and put in the freezer, beating every 30 minutes or so, until it is solid.

ginger cordial

adrak ka sherbet

This chilled drink has a biting, sharp flavour that is thirst quenching in hot weather, especially the steamy weeks before the monsoons. Ginger is one of the most ancient spices in India, and its medicinal properties are legendary. It is credited with soothing upset stomachs, and drinks like this are often sipped after a large meal as a digestive.

MAKES 4–6 GLASSES

70 g/2¹/₂ oz fresh root ginger, very finely chopped

¹/₂ tbsp finely grated lemon rind

1.2 litres/2 pints boiling water

2 tbsp fresh lemon juice, or to taste

4 tbsp caster sugar, or to taste

lemon and mint, to serve

1 Put the ginger in a heatproof bowl with the lemon rind. Pour over the boiling water, stir and leave to steep overnight.

2 Sieve the liquid into a large jug. Stir in the lemon juice and sugar, stirring until the sugar dissolves. Taste and add extra lemon juice and sugar, if you like. Serve decorated with lemon and mint.

ACCOMPANIMENTS

As is the style throughout Asia, side dishes in Indian meals have much more of a starring role than in western cuisines. Without the tradition of eating in a succession of courses, all the components of an Indian meal, from soup through to dessert, are served at once.

Traditionally meals are served *thali*-style on a large, round plate in the north or on a banana leaf in the South. Individual portions of a meat, poultry, seafood or a vegetarian dish are accompanied by rice and/or bread, a selection of fresh chutneys and a creamy yogurt Raita (see page 244) and are served in small bowls called *katoris* around the *thali*. And it is the rice dishes, breads and chutneys, which would be considered mere accompaniments in the West, that make Indian dining such an exciting feast of colours and tastes.

Regardless of whether the meal is 'veg' or 'non-veg', it always includes a starch in the form of rice or bread or both. Indian *roti*, or breads, not only have a nutritional role, but also replace knives and forks as most Indians eat with their fingers. The malleable texture of unleavened Chapatis (see page 236) and ghee-rich flaky Parathas (see page 239) make it easy to use a torn piece of bread to scoop up bite-sized portions of food. Both these breads are quickly cooked on flat griddles, eliminating the need for an oven, which many basic Indian kitchens don't include. Large, lightly leavened Naans (see page 235), on the other hand, are quickly baked on the inside of *tandoor* ovens, which means these are usually bought at food stalls or in restaurants.

The wheat-based breads of the north are served to a lesser extent in the south. There rice, rather than wheat, reigns supreme. Sometimes rice will be the only starch served at a meal, but at other meals the breads made from rice will be served, such as the

thin, crisp Dosas (see page 243) or the steamed *idlis*.

If any generalization is possible, it is that rice is served with more liquid, soup-like dishes such as Rasam (see page 71) and Sambhar (see page 82) and bread with the drier mixtures, such as Rogan Josh (see page 129).

For many Indians, especially southerners, and most foreigners, an Indian meal without rice is unimaginable. Mounds of rice, in numerous varieties and grades, are a feature of all Indian markets, and cooking it is second nature for home cooks. Long-grain Himalayan basmati rice is used for recipes in this book, but Patna rice, grown around the northern Indian town of the same name, is also suitable.

For an everyday rice recipe, try the Basmati Rice on page 26, but when there's time to make an effort, Spiced Basmati Rice (see page 232) has a fantastic fragrance and flavour that reflects Indian cooks' deft use of spices. Lemon Rice (see page 228) and Coconut Rice (see page 231) add the tastes of sunny southern India to any meal, while Fruit and Nut Pilaf (see page 227), with its spices, colourful dried fruit and rich pistachio nuts, evokes the lavish cooking of Moghul kitchens without the lengthy preparation of a biryani. A pilaf will transform a simple roast chicken into a maharajah's feast.

The real stars of Indian meals, however, are the chutneys, with their mixed textures and flavours. The word 'chutney' is an Anglicization of the Hindi word *chatni*, meaning 'freshly ground relish'. Like western relishes, chutneys can be raw or cooked,

finely chopped or chunky, and include many ingredients from fresh coconut, fruit and herbs, to seeds, spices, dals and so on. The possibilities are only limited by imagination. Mango chutney, familiar from all Indian restaurant and take-away meals, is a holdover from the British Raj. When colonial officers and their families returned home and meals seemed bland, a market developed for commercial brands that were shipped to Britain. These are still sold in

Overleaf Rice-farming is dominated by manual labour and rice fields have to be tended to almost daily

Mango chutney is a holdover from the British Raj

supermarkets, but the recipe on page 248 is a fresh, lighter version.

The other chutney recipes in this chapter reflect the diversity served in India. Coconut Sambal (see page 247) has a coarse texture, while Coriander Chutney (see page 245), with ginger and chilli, is a burst of fresh flavours. Chilli and Onion Chutney (see page 246) and Raita (see page 244) are the perfect accompaniments for *tandoori* recipes.

fruit and nut pilaf
shahi mewa pullao

A feast for your eyes as well as your palate! Religious festivals of all beliefs dot the calendar throughout the year in India, and on most of these occasions special food adds to the festivities. This colourful Moghul dish can be part of a vegetarian feast, and is favoured during the winter months in the north when fresh fruit isn't available. To mark an occasion, this would be served with Parathas (see page 239) rather than Chapatis (see page 236).

SERVES 4–6

225 g/8 oz basmati rice

450 ml/16 fl oz water

¹/₂ tsp saffron threads

1 tsp salt

30 g/1 oz Ghee (see page 253) or 2 tbsp vegetable or groundnut oil

55 g/2 oz blanched almonds

1 onion, thinly sliced

1 cinnamon stick, broken in half

seeds from 4 green cardamom pods

1 tsp cumin seeds

1 tsp black peppercorns, lightly crushed

2 bay leaves

3 tbsp finely chopped dried mango

3 tbsp finely chopped dried apricots

2 tbsp sultanas

55 g/2 oz pistachio nuts, chopped

1 Rinse the basmati rice in several changes of water until the water runs clear, then leave to soak for 30 minutes. Drain and set aside until ready to cook.

2 Boil the water in a small saucepan. Add the saffron threads and salt, remove from the heat and set aside to infuse.

3 Melt the ghee in a flameproof casserole or large saucepan with a tight-fitting lid over a medium-high heat. Add the almonds and stir them around until golden brown, then immediately use a slotted spoon to scoop them out of the casserole.

4 Add the onion to the casserole and fry, stirring frequently, for 5–8 minutes until golden, but not brown. Add the spices and bay leaves to the pan and stir them around for about 30 seconds.

5 Add the rice into the casserole and stir until the grains are coated with ghee. Add the saffron-infused water and bring to the boil. Reduce the heat to as low as possible, stir in the dried fruit and cover the casserole tightly. Simmer, without lifting the lid, for 8–10 minutes until the grains are tender and all the liquid is absorbed.

6 Turn off the heat and use 2 forks to mix the almonds and pistachios into the rice. Adjust the seasoning, if necessary. Re-cover the pan and leave to stand for 5 minutes*.

*cook's tip
If this dish, or any of the following rice recipes, are ready before you want to serve, place a clean tea towel between the rice and lid and leave the rice to stand for up to 20 minutes after you stir in the nuts in Step 6. The towel will absorb the steam and prevent the rice from becoming soggy.

228

lemon rice
nimbu bhaat

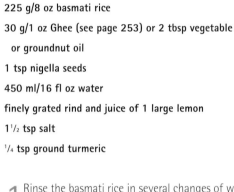

This colourful dish, popular in southern India, is ideal to serve with most fish dishes, as well as spiced meat dishes such as Lamb with Cauliflower (see page 141) and Lamb Shanks Marathani (see page 142).

SERVES 4–6

225 g/8 oz basmati rice

30 g/1 oz Ghee (see page 253) or 2 tbsp vegetable
 or groundnut oil

1 tsp nigella seeds

450 ml/16 fl oz water

finely grated rind and juice of 1 large lemon

1 1/2 tsp salt

1/4 tsp ground turmeric

1 Rinse the basmati rice in several changes of water until the water runs clear, then leave to soak for 30 minutes. Drain and set aside until ready to cook.

2 Melt the ghee in a flameproof casserole or large saucepan with a tight-fitting lid over a medium-high heat. Add the nigella seeds to the rice and stir until all the grains are coated in ghee. Add the water and bring to the boil.

3 Reduce the heat to as low as possible, stir in half the lemon juice, salt and turmeric and cover the casserole tightly. Simmer, without lifting the lid, for 8–10 minutes until the grains are tender and all the liquid is absorbed.

4 Turn off the heat and use 2 forks to mix the lemon rind and remaining juice into the rice. Adjust the seasoning, if necessary. Re-cover the casserole and leave the rice to stand for 5 minutes*.

*cook's tip

To make a lemon and cashew rice, melt the ghee as in Step 2, add 55 g/2 oz cashew nuts and stir them around for 30 seconds, or until golden brown. Immediately use a slotted spoon to remove them from the casserole so they do not become too brown. Add 1 teaspoon fenugreek seeds with the nigella seeds and continue with the recipe. Stir the cashew nuts into the rice in Step 4 with the lemon rind and juice, then re-cover the pan and leave to stand for 5 minutes. Serve garnished with chopped fresh mint.

Car ownership has been rising very quickly in India, and cars are now common even outside the main cities

Regarded as the 'fruit of the gods', coconut not only plays a major role in southern Indian kitchens, but also in Hindu religious ceremonies, where it can be used to symbolize a full, rich life. Fittingly, this dish is ideal for all special occasions.

SERVES 4–6

225 g/8 oz basmati rice

450 ml/16 fl oz water

60 g/2¼ oz creamed coconut

2 tbsp mustard oil*

1½ tsp salt

1 Rinse the basmati rice in several changes of water until the water runs clear, then leave to soak for 30 minutes. Drain and set aside until ready to cook.

2 Bring the water to the boil in a small saucepan, stir in the creamed coconut until it dissolves and then set aside.

3 Heat the mustard oil in a large frying pan or saucepan with a lid over a high heat until it smokes. Turn off the heat and leave the mustard oil to cool completely.

4 When you are ready to cook, reheat the mustard oil over a medium-high heat. Add the rice and stir until all the grains are coated in oil. Add the water with the dissolved coconut and bring to the boil.

5 Reduce the heat to as low as possible, stir in the salt and cover the pan tightly. Simmer, without lifting the lid, for 8–10 minutes until the grains are tender and all the liquid is absorbed.

6 Turn off the heat and use 2 forks to mix the rice. Adjust the seasoning, if necessary. Re-cover the pan and leave the rice to stand for 5 minutes.

coconut rice 231
thengai sadaam

*cook's tip

The mustard oil is heated and then cooled in Step 3 to reduce the pungency of its flavour. If you prefer to use vegetable or groundnut oil, you can skip this step.

Integral to Indian cooking, spices are often bought in bulk at the local market

232
spiced basmati rice
chunke hue chawal

This delicately flavoured dish comes from Rajasthan and has never fallen from favour since the days of Moghul rule. It is excellent to serve with lamb dishes.

SERVES 4–6

225 g/8 oz basmati rice

30 g/1 oz Ghee (see page 253) or 2 tbsp vegetable
  or groundnut oil

5 green cardamom pods, lightly cracked

5 cloves

2 bay leaves

$^1/_2$ cinnamon stick

1 tsp fennel seeds

$^1/_2$ tsp black mustard seeds

450 ml/16 fl oz water

$1^1/_2$ tsp salt

2 tbsp chopped fresh coriander

pepper

1 Rinse the basmati rice in several changes of water until the water runs clear, then leave to soak for 30 minutes. Drain and set aside until ready to cook.

2 Melt the ghee in a flameproof casserole or large saucepan with a tight-fitting lid over a medium-high heat. Add the spices and stir for 30 seconds. Stir the rice into the casserole so the grains are coated with ghee. Stir in the water and salt and bring to the boil.

3 Reduce the heat to as low as possible and cover the casserole tightly. Simmer, without lifting the lid, for 8–10 minutes until the grains are tender and all the liquid is absorbed.

4 Turn off the heat and use 2 forks to mix in the coriander. Adjust the seasoning, if necessary. Re-cover the pan and leave to stand for 5 minutes*.

*cook's tip

For spiced saffron basmati rice, lightly toast 1 teaspoon saffron threads in a dry frying pan over a medium-high heat until you can smell the aroma, then immediately tip them out of the pan. Bring the water to the boil while the rice soaks, stir in the saffron threads and the salt and set aside to infuse. Add the golden saffron-flavoured water to the recipe in Step 2, as above, and follow the remaining recipe.

The Indians use their extensive inland waterways to transport food and materials

These leavened breads have been baked in India since the days of Moghul rule, traditionally by slapping the rolled and shaped dough against the hot inside of a charcoal-heated tandoor oven. As it is unlikely you have a tandoor oven at home, you won't be able produce identical breads to those at your favourite Indian restaurant, but these are very close. Just be sure to preheat your oven with a baking sheet inside to its highest setting in plenty of time.

MAKES 10

900 g/2 lb strong white flour

1 tbsp baking powder

1 tsp sugar

1 tsp salt

300 ml/10 fl oz water, heated to 50°C/122°F

1 egg, beaten

55 g/2 oz Ghee (see page 253), melted, plus a little extra
  for rolling out and brushing

1 Sift the flour, baking powder, sugar and salt into a large mixing bowl and make a well in the centre. Mix together the water and egg, beating until the egg breaks up and is blended with the liquid.

2 Slowly add the liquid mixture to the well in the dry ingredients, using your fingers to draw in the flour from the side, until a stiff, heavy dough forms. Shape the dough into a ball and return it to the bowl.

3 Soak a clean tea towel in hot water, then wring it out and use it to cover the bowl, tucking the ends of the towel under the bowl. Set the bowl aside to let the dough rest for 30 minutes.

4 Turn out the dough on to a work surface brushed with melted ghee and flatten the dough. Gradually sprinkle the dough with the melted ghee and knead to work it in, little by little, until it is completely incorporated. Shape the dough into 10 equal balls.

5 Resoak the towel in hot water and wring it out again, then place it over the dough balls and leave them to rest and rise for 1 hour.

6 Meanwhile, put 1 or 2 baking sheets in the oven and preheat the oven to 230°C/450°F/ Gas Mark 8 or its highest setting.

7 Use a lightly greased rolling pin to roll the dough balls into teardrop shapes, about 3 mm/⅛ inch thick. Use crumpled kitchen paper to lightly rub the hot baking sheets with ghee. Arrange the naans on the baking sheets and bake for 5–6 minutes until they are golden brown and lightly puffed. As you take the naans out of the oven, brush with melted ghee and serve at once*.

*cook's tip

For garlic and nigella seed naans, scatter the dough just before it is baked with 3 very thinly sliced garlic cloves and 2 tablespoons nigella seeds. For sesame naans, sprinkle the dough just before it is baked with 2 tablespoons sesame seeds. For coriander naans, knead 55 g/2 oz finely chopped fresh coriander into the dough after the ghee is incorporated in Step 4.

chapatis
chapatis

The everyday bread for millions of Indians, eaten by
virtually everyone from the richest to the very poor.
The soft, malleable texture makes these flatbreads
ideal for mopping up 'gravies', as Indian sauces are
known, and for scooping up bite-sized portions of
food, doing away with knives and forks. Unleavened
chapatis are traditionally made with atta, a type of
Indian wholemeal flour that is sold in Asian food
shops and some large supermarkets, but ordinary
wholemeal flour is fine if you sift out the gritty
pieces of bran first. Indian cooks, who are very
accomplished at preparing these one after another
as a meal is being served, use a short, tapered rolling
pin that is thicker in the centre to shape the dough,
then cook it on a hot, flat griddle called a tava. An
ordinary rolling pin and frying pan, however, work
just as well.

MAKES 6

225 g/8 oz wholemeal flour, sifted,
   plus extra for dusting
$^1/_2$ tsp salt
150–200 ml/5–7 fl oz water
melted Ghee (see page 253), for brushing

1 Mix the flour and salt together in a large bowl and
make a well in the centre. Gradually stir in enough
water to make a stiff dough.

2 Turn out the dough on to a lightly floured surface
and knead for 10 minutes, or until it is smooth and
elastic. Shape the dough into a ball and place it in the
cleaned bowl, then cover with a damp tea towel and
leave to rest for 20 minutes.

3 Divide the dough into 6 equal pieces. Lightly flour
your hands and roll each piece of dough into a ball.
Meanwhile, heat a large, ungreased tava, frying pan or
griddle over a high heat until very hot and a splash of
water 'dances' when it hits the surface.

4 Working with 1 ball of dough at a time, flatten the
dough between your palms, then roll it out on a
lightly floured work surface into an 18-cm/7-inch
round. Slap the dough on to the hot pan and cook until
brown flecks appear on the bottom. Flip the dough over
and repeat on the other side*.

5 Flip the dough over again and use a bunched up
tea towel to press down all around the edge. This
pushes the steam in the chapati around, causing the
chapati to puff up. Continue cooking until the bottom
is golden brown, then flip over and repeat this step
on the other side.

6 Brush the chapati with melted ghee and serve,
then repeat with the remaining dough balls.
Chapatis are best served at once, as soon as they come
out of the pan, but they can be kept warm wrapped
in foil for about 20 minutes.

cook's tip

Do not be tempted to flip the chapatis more times
than specified above, or they will not puff up and
will become heavy. Indian cooks use their fingers to flip
the dough over in Steps 4 and 5, but unless you have
asbestos fingers, use a pair of tongs or a metal spatula.

These are shallow-fried, unleavened breads for special occasions and religious festivals. Made with lots of melted ghee, parathas have a flaky texture and are too rich for everyday meals — unless, of course, you don't worry about your waistline! For an Indian-style breakfast, try parathas with a bowl of thick yogurt.

MAKES 8

225 g/8 oz wholemeal flour, sifted,
  plus extra for dusting

½ tsp salt

150–200 ml/5–7 fl oz water

140 g/5 oz Ghee (see page 253), melted

1 Mix the flour and salt together in a large bowl and make a well in the centre. Gradually stir in enough water to make a stiff dough.

2 Turn out the dough on to a lightly floured surface and knead for 10 minutes, or until it is smooth and elastic. Shape the dough into a ball and place it in the cleaned bowl, then cover with a damp tea towel and leave to rest for 20 minutes.

3 Divide the dough into 8 equal pieces. Lightly flour your hands and roll each piece of dough into a ball.

4 Working with one ball of dough at a time, roll it out on a lightly floured work surface until it is a 13-cm/5-inch round. Brush the top of the dough with about 1½ teaspoons of the melted ghee. Fold the round in half to make a half-moon shape and brush the top again with melted ghee. Fold the half-moon shape in half again to make a triangle. Press the layers together.

5 Roll out the triangle on a lightly floured surface into a larger triangle that is about 18 cm/7 inches on each side. Flip the dough back and forth between your hands a couple of times, then cover with a damp cloth and continue until all the dough is shaped and rolled.

6 Meanwhile, heat a large, ungreased tava, frying pan or griddle over a high heat until very hot and a splash of water 'dances' when it hits the surface. Place a paratha in the pan and cook until bubbles appear on the surface.

7 Use tongs to flip the paratha over and brush the surface with melted ghee. Continue cooking until the bottom is golden brown, then flip the paratha over again and smear with more melted ghee. Use a wooden spoon or spatula to press down on the surface of the paratha so it cooks evenly.

8 Brush with more melted ghee and serve, then repeat with the remaining parathas. Parathas are best served at once, as soon as they come out of the pan, but they can be kept warm wrapped in foil for about 20 minutes.

Headgear is more than just a defence against heat and cold, it can be a symbol of religion, origin or social status

240

pooris
puris

These deep-fried breads puff up to look like balloons when they go into the hot oil, and are perfect for serving with most 'veg' and 'non-veg' curries. Children love watching these cooking. Pooris also make a traditional, if somewhat unexpected, accompaniment to Shrikhand with Pomegranate (see page 207). These will be made in huge quantities to serve at Hindu weddings and special occasions.

MAKES 12

225 g/8 oz wholemeal flour, sifted, plus extra for dusting

¹/₂ teaspoon salt

30 g/1 oz ghee, melted

100–150 ml/3¹/₂–5 fl oz water

vegetable or groundnut oil, for deep-frying

1 Put the flour and salt into a bowl and drizzle the ghee over the surface. Gradually stir in the water until a stiff dough forms.

2 Turn out the dough on to a lightly floured surface and knead for 10 minutes, or until it is smooth and elastic. Shape the dough into a ball and place it in the cleaned bowl, then cover with a damp tea towel and leave to rest for 20 minutes.

3 Divide the dough into 12 equal pieces and roll each into a ball. Working with one ball of dough at a time, flatten the dough between your palms, then thinly roll it out on a lightly floured work surface into a 13-cm/5-inch round. Continue until all the dough balls are rolled out.

4 Heat at least 7.5 cm/3 inches oil in a kadhai, wok, deep-fat fryer or large frying pan until it reaches 180°C/350°F, or until a cube of bread browns in 30 seconds. Drop one poori into the hot fat and fry for about 10 seconds, or until it puffs up. Use 2 large spoons to flip the poori over and spoon some hot oil over the top.

5 Use the 2 spoons to lift the poori from the oil and let any excess oil drip back into the pan. Drain the poori on crumpled kitchen paper and serve at once. Continue until all the pooris are fried, making sure the oil returns to the correct temperature before you add another poori.

*cook's tip
To make mini pooris to use in Bhel Poori (see page 44), roll out the dough as in Step 3, then use a lightly greased 4-cm/1¹/₂-inch biscuit cutter to stamp out smaller rounds.

In India, the streets are packed with vendors selling goods or their services

In southern India, these ultra-thin, crisp pancakes are served with Coriander Chutney or Coconut Sambal (see pages 245 and 247) for snacks, or rolled around a spicy potato mixture to make the popular Dosa Masala (see page 84), which is even served for breakfast. As dosas are cooked in a thin layer of ghee, they have a rich flavour. An experienced dosa maker will flip these on the hot tava, an Indian griddle, one after another without any apparent effort. For a novice dosa maker, however, it is a slower process. Try a practice batch first, and don't be tempted to flip a dosa before it has cooked long enough to become crisp on the bottom. It also helps to use the largest, flattest pan you have. A frying pan can be used, but a griddle or crêpe pan makes the job easier. In India, it's not uncommon to be served dosas that are up to 40 cm/16 inches across, but this recipe makes them in a more manageable size. Remember to start the batter a day in advance because it soaks overnight.

MAKES ABOUT 8 DOSAS

115 g/4 oz basmati rice, rinsed

70 g/2¹/₂ oz split black lentils (urad dal chilke)

¹/₄ tsp fenugreek seeds

125 ml/4 fl oz water

salt

30 g/1 oz Ghee (see page 253), melted

1 Bring a pan of salted water to the boil, add the basmati rice and boil for 5 minutes, then drain. Put the rice, split black lentils and fenugreek seeds in a bowl with water to cover and leave to soak overnight.

2 The next day, sieve the rice and lentils, reserving the soaking liquid. Put the rice and lentils in a food processor with 75 ml/2¹/₂ fl oz of the water and whiz until a smooth, sludgy grey paste forms. Slowly add the remaining water.

3 Cover the bowl with a tea towel that has been soaked in hot water and wrung out and leave to ferment in a warm place for 5–6 hours until small bubbles appear all over the surface.

4 Stir the mixture and add as much extra water as necessary to get a consistency of single cream. Add salt to taste. The amount of salt you need depends on how 'sour'-tasting the batter is.

5 Heat the flattest, largest pan you have over a high heat until a splash of water 'dances' when it hits the surface, then brush the surface with melted ghee. Put a ladleful of batter in the centre of the pan and use the bottom of the ladle to spread it out as thinly as possible in concentric circles, then leave it to cook for 2 minutes until it is golden brown and crisp on the bottom.

6 Flip the dosa over* and continue cooking for a further 2 minutes. Turn out of the pan and keep warm if you are going to wrap around a filling, or leave to cool. Continue until all the batter has been used.

*cook's tip
Although dosas look a little like French crêpes, they cook differently and do not slide around in the pan. To flip the dosa in Step 6 you need to slide a thin metal tool underneath to loosen it from the pan. A metal spatula can be used, but a clean paint scraper actually works more efficiently.

244 raita
raita

This is the all-purpose, everyday accompaniment that is served with almost any spicy dish and the variations are endless (see below). The creaminess of the yogurt and the coolness of the cucumber help to temper the heat of spicy dishes.

SERVES 4–6

1 large piece of cucumber, about 300 g/10½ oz, rinsed

1 teaspoon salt

400 ml/14 fl oz natural yogurt

½ teaspoon sugar

pinch of ground cumin

2 tablespoons chopped fresh coriander or mint

chilli powder, to garnish

1 Lay a clean tea towel flat on the work surface. Coarsely grate the unpeeled cucumber directly on to the towel. Sprinkle with ½ teaspoon of the salt, then gather up the towel and squeeze until all the excess moisture is removed from the cucumber.

2 Put the yogurt into a bowl and beat in the remaining ½ teaspoon of salt, along with the sugar and cumin. Stir in the grated cucumber. Taste and add extra seasoning, if you like. Cover and chill until ready to serve.

3 Stir in the chopped coriander and transfer to a serving bowl. Sprinkle with chilli powder and serve*.

* cook's tip
For a variation, stir in 2 deseeded and finely chopped tomatoes or 4 finely chopped spring onions with the coriander or mint. Ground coriander or ginger can also be added to taste. To make a banana raita, peel and slice 3 bananas directly into the yogurt, then stir in 2 deseeded and chopped fresh green chillies and 1 tablespoon garam masala. Add a little lemon rind and juice, if you like. Cover and chill until required, then stir in the chopped fresh coriander or mint just before serving.

coriander chutney
hare dhaniye ki chutney

This is an example of one of the uncooked, fresh-tasting chutneys that are served with every meal or snack throughout the day in Kerala, starting with breakfast. The bright green coriander, fresh coconut and chilli capture the flavours of the region.

MAKES ABOUT 225 G/8 OZ

1 1/2 tbsp lemon juice

1 1/2 tbsp water

85 g/3 oz fresh coriander leaves and stems, coarsely chopped

2 tbsp chopped fresh coconut

1 small shallot, very finely chopped

5-mm/1/4-inch piece of fresh root ginger, chopped

1 fresh green chilli, deseeded and chopped

1/2 tsp sugar

1/2 tsp salt

pinch of pepper

1 Put the lemon juice and water in a small food processor, add half the coriander and whiz until it is blended and a slushy paste forms. Gradually add the remaining coriander and whiz until it is all blended, scraping down the sides of the processor, if necessary. If you don't have a processor that will cope with this small amount, use a pestle and mortar, adding the coriander in small amounts.

2 Add the remaining ingredients and continue whizzing until they are all finely chopped and blended. Taste and adjust any of the seasonings, if you like. Transfer to a non-metallic bowl, cover and chill for up to 3 days before serving*.

*cook's tip

For a cooling coriander raita, stir 300 ml/10 fl oz natural yogurt into the chutney and chill for at least 1 hour before serving. Sprinkle with plenty of chopped fresh coriander just before serving.

246

chilli and onion chutney
mirch aur pyaaz ki chutney

For those who really like spicy hot food, this fresh chutney packs quite a punch. It's hot, zingy and can bring tears to your eyes if you don't deseed the chillies. Try this as an accompaniment to Tandoori Chicken (see page 156) or Chicken Tikka Masala (see page 161). Gujaratis will include the chilli seeds and serve this at all meals, eating it in the summer like a snack with poppadoms or Pooris (see page 240).

MAKES ABOUT 225 G/8 OZ

1–2 fresh green chillies, deseeded or not, to taste, and finely chopped

1 small fresh bird's eye chilli, deseeded or not, to taste, and finely chopped

1 tbsp white wine or cider vinegar

2 onions, finely chopped

2 tbsp fresh lemon juice

1 tbsp sugar

3 tbsp chopped fresh coriander, mint or parsley, or a combination of herbs

salt

chilli flower, to garnish

1 Put the chillies in a small non-metallic bowl with the vinegar, stir around and then drain. Return the chillies to the bowl and stir in the onions, lemon juice, sugar and herbs, then add salt to taste.

2 Leave to stand at room temperature or cover and chill for 15 minutes. Garnish with the chilli flower before serving*.

*cook's tip

For a chilli and onion raita, stir 300 ml/10 fl oz natural yogurt into the chutney mixture and chill for at least 1 hour. Stir before serving and sprinkle with fresh herbs.

Coconuts grow in abundance along the gently flowing backwaters in Kerala and slightly crunchy, fresh chutneys like this are served at many meals. Serve this with poppadoms as a snack or use it to accompany simply grilled fresh seafood. In Kerala and Tamil Nadu it is served with the crisp, thin Dosas (see page 243).

MAKES ABOUT 140 G/5 OZ

$^1/_2$ fresh coconut, about 115 g/4 oz of meat,
  or 125 g/4$^1/_2$ oz desiccated coconut

2 fresh green chillies, deseeded or not,
  to taste, and chopped

2.5-cm/1-inch piece of fresh root ginger, peeled
  and finely chopped

4 tbsp chopped fresh coriander

2 tbsp lemon juice, or to taste

2 shallots, very finely chopped

1 If you are using a whole coconut, use a hammer and nail to punch a hole in the 'eye' of the coconut, then pour out the water from the inside and reserve. Use the hammer to break the coconut in half, then peel half and chop.

2 Put the coconut and chillies in a small food processor and whiz for about 30 seconds until finely chopped. Add the ginger, coriander and lemon juice and whiz again.

3 If the mixture seems too dry, whiz in about 1 tablespoon coconut water or water. Stir in the shallots and serve at once, or cover and chill until required. This will keep its fresh flavour, covered, in the refrigerator for up to 3 days*.

coconut sambal
nariyal sambal

247

*cook's tip
For a punchier tasting chutney, stir in $^1/_2$ tablespoon black mustard seeds with the shallots. A little ground cumin is also a good addition.

248

mango chutney
aam ki chutney

This light, spiced chutney is about as far as one can get from the thick, overly sweet mango chutney in jars. It adds the sunny flavour of Goa and southern India to any Indian meal.

MAKES ABOUT 250 G/9 OZ

1 large mango, about 400 g/14 oz, peeled, stoned and finely chopped

2 tbsp lime juice

1 tbsp vegetable or groundnut oil

2 shallots, finely chopped

1 garlic clove, finely chopped

2 fresh green chillies, deseeded and finely sliced

1 tsp black mustard seeds

1 tsp coriander seeds

5 tbsp grated jaggery or light brown sugar

5 tbsp white wine vinegar

1 tsp salt

pinch of ground ginger

1 Put the mango in a non-metallic bowl with the lime juice and set aside.

2 Heat the oil in a large frying pan or saucepan over a medium-high heat. Add the shallots and fry for 3 minutes. Add the garlic and chillies and stir for a further 2 minutes, or until the shallots are soft, but not brown. Add the mustard and coriander seeds and then stir around.

3 Add the mango to the pan with the jaggery, vinegar, salt and ground ginger and stir around. Reduce the heat to its lowest setting and simmer for 10 minutes until the liquid thickens and the mango becomes sticky.

4 Remove from the heat and leave to cool completely. Transfer to an airtight container, cover and chill for 3 days before using. Store in the refrigerator and use within 1 week.

tamarind chutney 249
imli ki chutney

There isn't any mistaking the fresh, sour taste of
tamarind: it adds a distinctive flavour to many
dishes, especially those from southern India. More
like a sauce than a thick chutney, this sweet-and-
sour tasting mixture is essential to serve with Bhel
Poori (see page 44) and Vegetarian Samosas (see
page 40). It also goes particularly well with fried fish.

MAKES ABOUT 250 G/9 OZ

100 g/3¹/₂ oz tamarind pulp, chopped

450 ml/16 fl oz water

¹/₂ fresh bird's eye chilli, or to taste, deseeded
  and chopped

55 g/2 oz soft light brown sugar, or to taste

¹/₂ tsp salt

1 Put the tamarind and water in a heavy-based
saucepan over a high heat and bring to the boil.
Reduce the heat to the lowest setting and simmer
for 25 minutes, stirring occasionally to break up the
tamarind pulp, or until tender.

2 Tip the tamarind pulp into a sieve and use a wooden
spoon to push the pulp into the rinsed out pan.

3 Stir in the chilli, sugar and salt and continue
simmering for a further 10 minutes or until the
desired consistency is reached. Leave to cool slightly,
then stir in extra sugar or salt, to taste.

4 Leave to cool completely, then cover tightly
and chill for up to 3 days, or freeze.

*An Indian man stands against a dramatic
background of hills in Kumbulgarh*

250

chilli bon-bon
badi mirchi ka meetha achaa

Simple to make, this condiment adds an intriguing flavour to any simply grilled or roasted meat or seafood. 'Invented' by British army cooks during the Raj, you can still find this today on many Anglo-Indian tables.

MAKES 300 ML/10 FL OZ
300 ml/10 fl oz medium or dry sherry
1 or 2 fresh bird's eye chilli, to taste

1 Pour the sherry into a sterilized jar. Make several long slits in the chillies, then add them to the sherry. Seal the jar, shake well and set aside for at least 3 days before using. Store in the refrigerator and use within a month.

Men in India have traditionally grown moustaches as a sign of masculinity

'Garam' means 'hot' and 'masala' means 'mixed spices', so this is an aromatic mixture of hot spices, but not 'hot' as in the fiery, spicy hot meaning of the word, but rather as in warming to heat the body. Unlike most other spices and masala mixtures, garam masala is usually added towards the end of cooking for a savoury, fragrant taste. You can easily buy garam masala in supermarkets, Asian food shops and even corner shops, but if you do lots of Indian cooking it is fun to make your own mixture. Use this recipe as a starting point, but experiment with the quantities until you get a mixture that you like. Garam masala is almost always added in small amounts, so to prevent the flavour from dulling, do not make a large quantity. Indian cooks often make a fresh batch for each meal.

*cook's tip

If you don't have a small grinder that you use exclusively for spices, whiz a few pieces of torn white bread in the grinder after you use it for spices. The bread will absorb much of the residual aromas.

MAKES ABOUT 6 TABLESPOONS

2 bay leaves, crumbled

2 cinnamon sticks, broken in half

seeds from 8 green cardamom pods

2 tbsp cumin seeds

1¹/₂ tbsp coriander seeds

1¹/₂ tsp black peppercorns

1 tsp cloves

¹/₄ tsp ground cloves

1 Heat a dry frying pan over a high heat until a splash of water 'dances' when it hits the surface. Reduce the heat to medium, add the bay leaves, cinnamon sticks, cardamom pods, cumin seeds, coriander seeds, peppercorns and cloves and dry-roast, stirring constantly, until the cumin seeds look dark golden brown and you can smell the aromas.

2 Immediately tip the spices out of the pan and leave to cool. Use a spice grinder* or pestle and mortar to grind the spices to a fine powder. Stir in the ground cloves. Store in an airtight container for up to 2 months.

252 paneer
paneer

For India's millions of vegetarians, this firm white cheese is a main source of daily protein. Although paneer has a bland flavour on its own, it is similar to Asian tofu in that it absorbs flavours when cooked with other ingredients. In all of India, except in the South, paneer is used in both savoury and sweet dishes. It is often partnered with pulses and vegetables, and its firm texture means it is also ideal for grilling and roasting. Fresh paneer is sold in Asian food shops, but it is straightforward to make at home.

MAKES ABOUT 350 G/12 OZ

2.2 litres/4 pints of milk

6 tbsp lemon juice

1 Pour the milk into a large, heavy-based saucepan over a high heat and bring to a full boil. Remove the pan from the heat and stir in the lemon juice. Return the pan to the heat and continue boiling for a further minute until the curds and whey separate and the liquid is clear.

2 Remove the pan from the heat and set aside for an hour or so, until the milk is completely cool. Meanwhile, line a sieve set over a bowl with a piece of muslin large enough to hang over the edge.

3 Pour the cold curds and whey* into the muslin, then gather up the edges and squeeze out all the excess moisture.

4 Use a piece of string to tightly tie the muslin around the curds in a ball. Put the ball in a bowl and place a plate on top. Place a can of beans or tomatoes on the plate to weigh down the curds, then leave for at least 12 hours in the refrigerator. The curds will press into a compact mass that can be cut. The paneer will keep for up to 3 days in the refrigerator.

*cook's tip

The whey by-product of paneer-making can be discarded, but clever Indian cooks add it to the cooking water for vegetables or lentils.

The traditional rich flavour of many Indian dishes, especially those from the northern regions, comes, at least in part, from cooking with ghee, an Indian form of clarified butter. To make ghee, the golden butter fat and milk solids are separated over heat, and then simmered a little longer until the milk solids turn light brown, which develops a slightly nutty flavour. It is this nutty flavour that distinguishes ghee from clarified butter in the West. Ghee is the cooking fat of choice for many Indian cooks because of its flavour and because it doesn't burn at high temperatures. But, alas, its high cholesterol content means it is slowly being replaced on an everyday basis by a vegetable oil, such as sunflower or groundnut. This is why many recipes in this book list oil as an alternative to ghee. Supermarkets and, of course, Asian food shops sell tubs of ghee, but when you don't cook Indian every day and want an authentic flavour, it is easy to make.

MAKES ABOUT 200 G/7 OZ
250 g/9 oz butter

1 Melt the butter in a large, heavy-based saucepan over a medium heat and continue simmering until a thick foam appears on the surface.

2 Continue simmering, uncovered, for about 15–20 minutes*, or until the foam separates and the milk solids settle on the bottom and the liquid becomes clear and golden.

3 Meanwhile, line a sieve with a piece of muslin and place the sieve over a bowl. Slowly pour the liquid through the muslin, without disturbing the milk solids at the bottom of the pan. Discard the milk solids.

4 Leave the ghee to cool, then transfer it to a smaller container, cover and chill. It will keep in the refrigerator for up to 4 weeks, or it can be frozen.

*cook's tip
Watch the simmering ghee closely in Step 2 because the milk solids on the base of the pan can burn quickly.

index

Aam Ki Chutney 248
Aam Ki Lassi 213
Adrak Ka Sherbet 217
Akoori 89
Alcohol 197
Aloo Gobi 103
Aloo Ka Raita 52
Aloo Mattar Samosa 40–1
Asafoetida 28
Aubergine
    Cauliflower, Aubergine
        and Green Bean Korma 90
    Tomato-stuffed Aubergines 94

Badi Mirchi Ka Meetha Achaa 250
Balti dishes
    Balti Beef 155
    Balti Fish Curry 181
Banana leaves 26
Basmati rice *see* Rice
Beans *see* Green Beans
Beef
    Balti Beef 155
    Beef Madras 152
    Kheema Matar 151
Bhajis
    Okra Bhaji 106
    Onion Bhaji 38
Bhangde Lonchen 186
Bharwan Baingan Tamattari 94
Bhel Poori 32, 44
Bhindi Ki Sabzi 106
Bhuna Gosht 155
Bhuni Pattagobhi 87
Biryani, Lamb 126–7
Black Dal 113
Bread 16, 220
    Bhel Poori 32, 44
    Chapatis 16, 220, 236
    Indian Bread Pudding 206
    Naans 16, 220, 235
    Parathas 16, 220, 239
    Pooris 240
    Prawn Pooris 185
Butter Chicken 158

Cabbage, Spiced Balti Cabbage 87
Cachumber 64
Cardamom 23, 28
Carrots
    Carrot Halva 203

Gujarat Carrot Salad 65
Cashew nuts 24
Cauliflower
    Aloo Gobi 103
    Cauliflower, Aubergine
        and Green Bean Korma 90
    Golden Cauliflower Pakoras 42
    Lamb with Cauliflower 141
Chaat 20, 22, 32
Champ Tilwale 134
Chapatis 16, 220, 236
Chatpate Channe 67
Chhole Tamattar 93
Chicken
    Butter Chicken 158
    Chicken Jalfrezi 164
    Chicken Tikka 55
    Chicken Tikka Masala 13, 161
    Kashmiri Chicken 162–3
    Quick Chicken Curry with Mushrooms
        and Beans 160
    Tandoori Chicken 156–7
Chickpeas 16, 76
    Bhel Poori 32, 44
    Chickpeas with Spiced Tomatoes 93
    Chilli Chickpea Salad 67
Chilli
    Chilli Bon-bon 250
    Chilli Chickpea Salad 67
    Chilli and Onion Chutney 246
    chilli powder 28
    Chilli-yogurt Mushrooms 107
Chillies 23, 24, 28
Christmas 13
Chunke Hue Chawal 232
Chutney 220, 223
    Chilli Bon-bon 250
    Chilli and Onion Chutney 246
    Coconut Sambal 247
    Coriander Chutney 178, 245
    Mango Chutney 223, 248
    Tamarind Chutney 249
Cinnamon 29
Cloves 29
Cocktail Crab Cakes 62
Coconut 23, 26
    Coconut Rice 231
    Coconut Sambal 247
    cream 26
    Green Beans with Mustard Seeds and
Coconut 109

milk 26
    Spiced Pumpkin and Coconut 88
Coffee 24
Coriander 26, 29
    Coriander Chutney 178, 245
    Coriander Lamb Kebabs 133
Crab
    Cocktail Crab Cakes 62
    Malabar Hill Crab Salad 66
Cumin 29
Curry 13–14
    Balti Fish Curry 181
    Goan-style Seafood Curry 182
    Quick Chicken Curry with Mushrooms
        and Beans 160
Curry leaves 23, 26

Dahi Pamplet 189
Dairy products 10, 16
    see *also* Paneer; Yogurt
Dalchini 24
Dals 16, 23, 76
    see *also* Lentils; Pulses
Dhansak, Lamb 138
Divali 10
Dopiaza, Lamb 137
Dosas 23, 220, 243
    Dosa Masala 84

Eggs
    Parsi Scrambled Eggs 20, 89
Eguru Kosumalli 66

Fenugreek 26–7
Fish 10, 16, 20, 22, 24, 168, 170
    Balti Fish Curry 181
    Fish Pakoras 190
    hilsa 20, 22
    Pickled Mackerel 186
    Pomfret in Chilli Yogurt 189
    Steamed Fish with Coriander
        Chutney 178
Frans Bean Raiwali 109
Fruit and Nut Pilaf 227

Gajar Ka Halwa 203
Gajar Nu Salat 65
Garam Masala 16, 251
Garlic 16, 79
    Garlic and Ginger Paste 27
Ghati Gosht 142

Ghee 16, 253
Ginger 27
    Garlic and Ginger Paste 27
    Ginger Cordial 217
Goa Che Nalla Chi Kadi 182
Goan-style Seafood Curry 182
Goat 120
Gobhi Gosht 141
Gobhi Ka Pakora 42
Golden Cauliflower Pakoras 42
Gosht Biryani 126–7
Gosht Dhansak 138
Gosht Dopiaza 137
Gosht Hara Kabab 133
Gosht Pasanda 130
Gosht Vindaloo 148
Green Beans
    Cauliflower, Aubergine and Green Bean
      Korma 90
    Green Beans with Mustard Seeds
      and Coconut 109
    Quick Chicken Curry with Mushrooms
      and Beans 160
Greens 16
    see *also* Cabbage; Spinach
Ground Mango 29
Gujarat Carrot Salad 65

Haldi Dahi Ka Shorba 72
Hare Dhaniye Ki Chutney 245
Hot Tomato Raita 86

Imli Ki Chutney 249
Indian Bread Pudding 206

Jaggery 27
Jalfrezi, Chicken 164
Jhinga Aur Annanas Tikka 51
Jhinga Puri 185

Kaddu Aur Nariyal Ki Sabzi 88
Kashmiri Chicken 162–3
Kebabs, Coriander Lamb Kebabs 133
Kekda Tikki 62
Kele Ke Chips 59
Kesar Badaam Kulfi 204
Khandvi 16, 47
Khatta-Meetha Mewa 43
Khatti Meethi Daal 114
Kheema Matar 151
Kheer 200
Khichdee 117
Kitchri 117
Korma
    Cauliflower, Aubergine and Green Bean
      Korma 90

Kulfi 32, 197
    Saffron and Almond Kulfi 204

Lamb
    Coriander Lamb Kebabs 133
    Kheema Matar 151
    Lamb Biryani 126–7
    Lamb with Cauliflower 141
    Lamb Dhansak 138
    Lamb Dopiaza 137
    Lamb Pasanda 130
    Lamb Shanks Marathani 142
    Rogan Josh 129
    Sesame Lamb Chops 134
Lassi 16, 32, 197
    Mango Lassi 213
    Salt Lassi 212
Lemon Rice 228
Lentils 76
    Black Dal 113
    Kitchri 117
    Sambhar 82
    Spinach and Lentils 110
    Sweet-and-sour Lentils 114
    see *also* Dals

Maah Ki Daal 113
Machchli Masala 181
Machchli Pakora 190
Madras Potatoes 104
Madrasi aloo 104
Madrasi Gosht 152
Malabar Hill Crab Salad 66
Mango
    Ground Mango 29
    Mango Chutney 223, 248
    Mango Lassi 213
Masala Dosa 84
Masala Jhinga Aur Kakdi 48
Masala Tea 214
Masalewali Chai 214
Matar Paneer 100
Memsahib's Mulligatawny Soup 68
Mint 27
Mirch Aur Pyaaz Ki Chutney 246
Moghuls 13, 15, 23, 120, 194
Mullagatanni 68
Murgh Jalfrezi 164
Murgh Kashmiri 162–3
Murgh Makhani 158
Murgh Mushroom Rasedaar 160
Murgh Tikka 55
Murgh Tikka Makhani 161
Mushroom Dahiwale 107
Mushrooms
    Chilli-yogurt Mushrooms 107

Quick Chicken Curry with Mushrooms
    and Beans 160
Mussels with Mustard Seeds
    and Shallots 177
Mustard oil 27
Mustard Seeds 23, 29
    Green Beans with Mustard Seeds
      and Coconut 109
    Mussels with Mustard Seeds
      and Shallots 177
Mattar Paneer 100

Naans 16, 220, 235
Namkeen Lassi 212
Nariyal Sambal 247
Nigella seeds 29
Nimbu Bhaat 228
Nuts
    cashew nuts 24
    Fruit and Nut Pilaf 227
    Pistachio and Almond Shake 216
    Saffron and Almond Kulfi 204
    Sweet and Spicy Nuts 43

Okra Bhaji 106
Onions 16, 79
    Mussels with Mustard Seeds
      and Shallots 177
    Onion Bhaji 38
    Onion and Tomato Salad 64

Paatrani Machchi 178
Pakoras
    Fish Pakoras 190
    Golden Cauliflower Pakoras 42
Palak Daal 110
Panch phoron 23
Paneer 16, 79, 252
    Matar Paneer 100
    Paneer Tikka 60–1
Parathas 16, 220, 239
Parsi Scrambled Eggs 20, 89
Pasanda, Lamb 130
Patna rice *see* Rice
Payasam 201
Phal Ki Chaat 210
Pickled Mackerel 186
Pilaf 220
    Fruit and Nut Pilaf 227
Pista-badaam Doodh 216
Pistachio and Almond Shake 216
Plantain Chips 59
Pomegranate, Shrikhand
    with Pomegranate 207
Pomfret 20
    Pomfret in Chilli Yogurt 189

256

Pooris 240
   Bhel Poori 32, 44
   Prawn Pooris 185
Pork
   Pork Vindaloo 148
   Railroad Pork and Vegetables 147
Potatoes
   Aloo Gobi 103
   Bhel Poori 32, 44
   Dosa Masala 84
   Madras Potatoes 104
   Raita Potatoes 52
   Sambhar 82
Prawns
   Prawn and Pineapple Tikka 51
   Prawn Pooris 185
   Spicy Prawns with Cucumber 48
   Tandoori Prawns 174
Pulses 10, 16, 76
   see also Chickpeas; Dals; Lentils
Pumpkin, Spiced Pumpkin and Coconut 88
Puris 240
Pyaaz Pakora 38

Railroad Pork and Vegetables 147
Raita 244
   Raita Potatoes 52
Ramadan 10, 13
Rasam 71
Religion and food 10, 13, 16, 20, 23, 76
Rice 10, 14, 16, 20, 23, 220
   basmati 14, 20, 26, 220
   Coconut Rice 231
   Dosa Masala 84
   dosas 23, 220, 243
   Fruit and Nut Pilaf 227
   Kitchri 117
   Lemon Rice 228
   patna 14, 220
   Spiced Basmati Rice 232
Rogan Josh 129

Saag Paneer 99
Sabzi Gosht 147
Sabzi Ka Korma 90
Saffron 29
   Saffron and Almond Kulfi 204
Salads
   Chilli Chickpea Salad 67
   Gujarat Carrot Salad 65
   Malabar Hill Crab Salad 66
   Onion and Tomato Salad 64
Salt Lassi 212
Sambhar 82–3
Samosas, Vegetarian 40–1
Scrambled Eggs 20, 89

Seafood 10, 16, 23, 24, 168
   Cocktail Crab Cakes 62
   Goan-style Seafood Curry 182
   Malabar Hill Crab Salad 66
   Mussels with Mustard Seeds
     and Shallots 177
   Prawn and Pineapple Tikka 51
   Prawn Pooris 185
   Spicy Prawns with Cucumber 48
   Tandoori Prawns 174
Sesame Lamb Chops 134
Shahi Mewa Pullao 227
Shahi Tukda 206
Shrikhand Anaari 207
Shrikhand with Pomegranate 207
Silver foil 27
Soup
   Memsahib's Mulligatawny Soup 68
   Rasam 71
   Turmeric Yogurt Soup 72
Spiced Balti Cabbage 87
Spiced Basmati Rice 232
Spiced Fruit Salad 210
Spiced Pumpkin and Coconut 88
Spices 10, 23, 28–9
Spicy Prawns with Cucumber 48
Spinach 16
   Spinach and Lentils 110
   Spinach and Paneer 99
Steamed dishes 23
   Steamed Fish with Coriander
     Chutney 178
Sweet and Spicy Nuts 43
Sweet-and-sour Lentils 114

Tamarind 23, 27
   Tamarind Chutney 249
Tamattar Ka Raita 86
Tandoor 16, 120
Tandoori cooking 13, 15–16
   Tandoori Chicken 156–7
   Tandoori Prawns 174
Tandoori Jhinga 174
Tandoori Murgh 156–7
Tea 14, 32, 197
   Masala Tea 214
Thengai Sadaam 231
Tissario Kadugu 177
Tomato
   Chickpeas with Spiced Tomatoes 93
   Hot Tomato Raita 86
   Onion and Tomato Salad 64
   Tomato-stuffed Aubergines 94
Turmeric 23, 29
   Turmeric Yogurt Soup 72

Vegetarian dishes 76, 79
   Aloo Gobi 103
   Bhel Poori 32, 44
   Black Dal 113
   Cauliflower, Aubergine and Green Bean
     Korma 90
   Chickpeas with Spiced Tomatoes 93
   Chilli Chickpea Salad 67
   Chilli-yogurt Mushrooms 107
   Dosa Masala 84
   Golden Cauliflower Pakoras 42
   Green Beans with Mustard Seeds
     and Coconut 109
   Gujarat Carrot Salad 65
   Hot Tomato Raita 86
   Khandvi 16, 47
   Kitchri 117
   Madras Potatoes 104
   Matar Paneer 100
   Okra Bhaji 106
   Onion Bhaji 38
   Onion and Tomato Salad 64
   Paneer Tikka 60–1
   Parsi Scrambled Eggs 89
   Plantain Chips 59
   Raita Potatoes 52
   Rasam 71
   Sambhar 82–3
   Samosas 40–1
   Spiced Balti Cabbage 87
   Spiced Pumpkin and Coconut 88
   Spinach and Lentils 110
   Spinach and Paneer 99
   Sweet and Spicy Nuts 43
   Sweet-and-sour Lentils 114
   Tomato-stuffed Aubergines 94
Vegetarians 10, 16, 76
Vindaloo, Pork 148

Yogurt 16, 27
   Chilli-Yogurt Mushrooms 107
   Pomfret in Chilli Yogurt 189
   Raita 244
   Shrikhand with Pomegranate 207
   Turmeric Yogurt Soup 72